The Courage to Be
YOURSELF

The **Courage** to Be
YOURSELF

True Stories by Teens About Cliques, Conflicts, and Overcoming Peer Pressure

Edited by Al Desetta, M.A.,
with Educators for Social Responsibility

EDUCATORS FOR **SOCIAL RESPONSIBILITY**

free spirit
PUBLISHING®

Library of Congress Cataloging-in-Publication Data
The courage to be yourself : true stories by teens about cliques, conflicts, and overcoming peer pressure / edited by Al Desetta.
  p. cm.
  Includes index.
  ISBN 1-57542-185-2
1. Teenagers—Social conditions. 2. Adolescent psychology. 3. Interpersonal relations in adolescence. 4. Self-realization.
5. Teenagers—Case studies. I. Desetta, Al.
  HQ796.C8235 2005
  305.235—dc22   2005005173
eBook ISBN: 978-1-57542-854-3

"My Group Home Scapegoat" and "Who's the Real 'Problem Child'?" reprinted from *The Heart Knows Something Different: Teenage Voices from the Foster Care System*, by Youth Communication, copyright © 1996 by Youth Communication/New York Center, Inc., by permission of Persea Books, Inc., New York. All rights reserved. "Princess Oreo Speaks Out" (originally "Princess Oreo") reprinted from *Fighting the Monster: Teens Write About Confronting Emotional Challenges and Getting Help*, by Youth Communication, copyright © 2004 by Youth Communication/New York Center, Inc., by permission of Youth Communication/New York Center, Inc. "Gay On the Block" (originally "Gay On the Block, Gay in the Group Home") and "My Boy Wanted a Boyfriend" (originally "My Boy Had a Boyfriend") reprinted from *In the System and in the Life: A Guide for Teens and Staff to the Gay Experience in Foster Care*, by Youth Communication, copyright © 2003 by Youth Communication/New York Center, Inc., by permission of Youth Communication/New York Center, Inc. "She's Cool, She's Funny, She's Gay" (originally "Coming Out to Mom") reprinted from *Out With It: Gay and Straight Teens Write About Homosexuality*, by Youth Communication, copyright © 1996 by Youth Communication/New York Center, Inc., by permission of Youth Communication/New York Center, Inc. "Losing My Friends to Weed" excerpted from *The Struggle to Be Strong: True Stories by Teens About Overcoming Tough Times* edited by Al Desetta, M.A., and Sybil Wolin, Ph.D., copyright © 2000. Used with permission from Free Spirit Publishing Inc., Minneapolis, MN; 1-866-703-7322. All rights reserved.

In the following stories, names and/or identifying details have been changed: *Getting Guys off My Back, Nasty Girls, At Home in the Projects, My Group Home Scapegoat*.

"Sixteen Going on Seventeen" lyrics by Oscar Hammerstein II, music by Richard Rodgers, from the motion picture *The Sound of Music*, copyright © 1965, RCA/Ariola International, New York, NY.

Reading Level Grades 7 & Up; Interest Level Ages 13 & Up;
Fountas & Pinnell Guided Reading Level Z

15 14 13 12 11 10 9 8
Printed in the United States of America
S18860313

Free Spirit Publishing Inc.
Minneapolis, MN
(612) 338-2068
help4kids@freespirit.com
www.freespirit.com

Printed on
recycled paper

including 50%
post-consumer waste

green press
INITIATIVE

DEDICATION

To the teens and staff at Youth Communication, New York, for their work in giving a voice to young people for 25 years.

ACKNOWLEDGMENTS

First and foremost, my thanks to Keith Hefner, founder and executive director of Youth Communication, for his generosity in making available the stories in *The Courage to Be Yourself,* without which this book would not have been possible. Since 1980, Keith has directed a nationally recognized writing program for teens that publishes two award-winning magazines where these stories originally appeared—*New Youth Connections* and *Represent* (the latter written by youth in foster care). The eloquent and courageous essays that follow are a tribute to Keith's vision that young people should have a voice and his dedicated leadership in making that vision a reality for the last 25 years.

I am also greatly indebted to the exceptional skill, patience, and sensitivity of the Youth Communication editors who worked with the authors in this book to craft their stories. My thanks to: Rachel Blustain, Andrea Estepa, Clarence Haynes, Kendra Hurley, Philip Kay, Nora McCarthy, and Tamar Rothenberg. And my thanks to all Youth Communication staff who have supported their efforts.

The Courage to Be Yourself, and the *Leader's Guide* that accompanies it, are the products of a collaboration with Educators for Social Responsibility (ESR), the national organization that teaches young people creative and productive ways of resolving conflict. Sherrie Gammage, senior program associate at ESR, and Jeff Perkins, director of publications and marketing, gave valuable assistance in the editorial development of this anthology. I am grateful to work with such skilled and knowledgeable colleagues. Thanks to Larry Dieringer, executive director of ESR, for his efforts in bringing together this collaboration, and to Tom Roderick, executive director of ESR, Metropolitan, for sharing helpful information at the start of the project.

As always, the staff at Free Spirit Publishing has been both a pleasure and a privilege to work with. I am grateful to Judy Galbraith, publisher and president, for envisioning the need for this book and providing me with the opportunity to work on it. Margie Lisovskis, editorial director, deftly guided the overall process. And giving new life to the expression "last but not least," I want to thank my editor, Eric Braun, who asked the perceptive questions that made this a better book.

—Al Desetta

CONTENTS

Introduction:
CONFLICT AND COURAGE

Dwan Carter, 17, is proud to be African American. But because she listens to rock music, uses big vocabulary words instead of slang, and can't dance very well, Dwan's friends—and even her family—accuse her of not being black enough. The teasing and judging hurt, but Dwan doesn't believe that being black means she has to behave in certain ways and not others. She wants to be accepted just for who she is.

Dwan's story, "Princess Oreo Speaks Out," is one of 26 true stories by teens in *The Courage to Be Yourself*. Every writer in this book has faced peer pressure, teasing, bullying, exclusion, or just feeling "different" from everyone else. Nadishia gets harassed because she doesn't wear the latest designer clothes. Rana, who is Arab American, becomes the target of hate after the September 11th terrorist attacks. Cassandra's friends make fun of her for sitting with kids from other races in the school cafeteria. Yen gets teased for being Chinese, Jeremiah for being gay, and Jamel for not wanting to smoke marijuana. One anonymous teen is so afraid of being ridiculed for liking musicals that he keeps his tastes a secret. All these writers ask themselves tough questions: Why does everyone have such a problem with me? How come people can't accept me for who I am? Is it okay to be different? Should I change myself to fit in?

The Courage to Be Yourself is about the conflicts that teens go through when they get labeled and judged because they seem different. Differences can be threatening. Most people trust what they're familiar with and fear the unfamiliar. These fears and conflicts are especially common in school, where cliques are all over. That's why many of these stories take place in school.

Esther, 17, author of "A Stranger in a Strange School," moved to the United States from India just in time for eighth grade. On

1

her first day of school in the United States, she sees a boy with blond hair and blue eyes and thinks he's "the weirdest-looking person alive." To most Americans, blond hair and blue eyes are not unusual, but Esther never saw a person like that in India. As she writes, "I thought everyone would look like me."

Esther begins to feel that everyone else is normal and she's the weird one. But the labels "normal" and "weird"—like most labels—don't tell the whole story. They don't tell us what's most important about a person. Instead, labels are an easy way of judging people without making the effort to get to know them. By the end of her story, Esther learns that important fact. "Who's to say what's normal and what's weird?" she writes.

Still, labels are hard to avoid. You make statements by the friends you choose, where you sit at lunch, where you hang out, the clothes you wear, the music you listen to, the way you talk, and even the way you walk. At the same time, people make assumptions about you because of things you don't choose or have control over, such as your race, physical appearance, where you live, or your sexual orientation. People are quick to judge by using labels because, in a sense, what else do they have to go by? We're all limited by our own points of view and the groups we belong to—our families, neighborhoods, schools, and cultural backgrounds.

It's okay, and even important, to belong to a group, because groups help people feel secure. But it's important not to let groups define individuals. When race or dress or sexual orientation—or another label—is all you know about an individual, that individual becomes less of a person. And that can lead to conflict.

Reading The Courage to Be Yourself will help you deal with conflict. These true stories were written by teens who were part of a youth journalism program in New York City called Youth Communication. Their stories were originally published in two magazines, New Youth Connections and Represent, so that other teens could be helped by what they wrote and realize they were not alone. A group called Educators for Social Responsibility (ESR), who are experts in teaching teens about resolving conflicts peacefully, helped choose the stories. ESR believes that one way teens can solve conflicts with each other is by understanding and respecting the differences among themselves. And part of that process involves understanding and respecting yourself.

WHO'S TO SAY WHAT'S NORMAL AND WHAT'S WEIRD?

The importance of accepting who you are is a common theme in these stories. Being comfortable with yourself doesn't guarantee that others will accept you. But the more comfortable you are with yourself, the more likely you'll be to accept others—and to deal with people who can't accept you.

Conflict is messy and painful and can't always be avoided. But it can also present you with an opportunity to learn something new and positive about yourself. Conflict can:

- help you discover strengths you didn't know you had and open yourself to new people, experiences, and points of view

- lead you to question your assumptions about a person or group and befriend someone you never expected to be friends with, and

- teach you how to make wiser choices the next time conflict comes your way.

The teens in this book have used conflict to become stronger, better people, and you can too.

The choices and changes they made weren't easy—their stories don't always end happily, with all difficulties solved. Some writers lose friends who mean a lot to them, others continue to be teased and harassed, and many continue to struggle with difficult emotions. There are no magic solutions to the problems they write about.

But that is also the value of *The Courage to Be Yourself*. Because these stories don't provide easy answers (or come from adults), you can trust them. These teens have experienced real problems—and faced them and dealt with them—showing ways you can do the same. All the writers in this book have displayed great courage and strength in confronting teasing, bullying, and peer pressure, and in coming to terms with their own stereotypes and preconceptions.

You don't have much control over how others view you. But you do have control over how you view yourself, how you view and treat others, and how you react to the way they view and treat you. We all have positive choices to make, even at the most difficult times. These stories prove it.

THINKING ABOUT THE STORIES

At the end of each story, you'll find two or three questions under the heading "Think About It." These are to help you think about what you've just read and to relate the writer's experience to your own life. Take a few moments to reflect on the questions.

And if you feel like it, jot down some thoughts in reaction to the questions. You don't have to write a lot—a few sentences can help you clarify your reactions to what you read.

Maybe you've had the experience of keeping a diary or journal, or writing letters. If so, you know that writing helps you learn things about yourself and gives you a good way to deal with difficult emotions. Putting feelings on paper can help you gain more control over them.

Just thinking about the questions is enough. But if you feel the urge to do so, writing responses to the questions may deepen your enjoyment and understanding of the book.

NOTE: Some stories in this book include slang or unfamiliar words. The glossary on page 125 provides definitions of some of these words.

Each story ends with information about the author. In some cases, Youth Communication has lost contact with the writers. When possible, however, we've briefly described where the author is now and what he or she is doing.

THE STORIES

IN DeFeNSe OF MISFITS

By Andrea Uva

I grew up in a rich, white suburb. Whenever I heard about kids going into their high schools and shooting other kids, I felt I understood the anger of the killers. Their towns reminded me of my town. Their high schools reminded me of my high school.

Fathers in my town are mostly successful businessmen and commute to the city to work. The wives do not have many responsibilities. They don't have jobs and the housework is done by paid help. They fill their days with volunteering and school-related clubs like the Parent-Teacher Committee. They are the typical "soccer moms" of America.

Adults here are constantly talking about and comparing their children. At an early age, children learn that they are being watched not only by their own parents, but also by their friends' parents. There's a lot of pressure on kids to excel both in class and on the playing field.

The smartest, most beautiful, and most athletic kids are considered the best. Literally, the blonder the hair, the leaner the figure, the better. Parents pass their belief in these stereotypes on to their children early, and those stereotypes become part of their children's minds.

Most kids fit the ideal description, so they hung out together in one big clique (called "the preps"). The kids in the clique excluded the kids they labeled "strange" because of their appearance or manner.

As far back as middle school I was considered one of the strange kids, mostly because I wasn't athletic and was thought unattractive. My friends didn't fit in either.

There was one big group of friends who always hung out together at school, and I was out of it even though I tried to fit in. At lunch one day in the cafeteria, I saw a girl who was in some of my classes and who I thought liked me. I said hello to her and sat down next to her.

Without saying a word, but with a smile on her face, she picked up her lunch bag and moved one seat away from me. I was humiliated, but I didn't move to another table.

When I read about school shootings, I understood why some kids started their rampages in the cafeteria. That is where kids who don't fit in are treated the worst. It's a place without adult supervision, where kids can pick whom they hang out with and whom they ignore.

In my high school, the large cafeteria (called the Lounge) was split in half. The South Lounge was always packed and almost everyone sat there. The North Lounge was almost empty. It was where the "dorks" and "losers" ate.

It frustrated me that during lunch, my friends would sit in the "Loser Lounge." They seemed to accept that they were not cool enough.

My freshman year, I still felt desperate to be liked. I had friends, but what I really wanted was to be part of "the group." I didn't think I was that different from anybody else. I didn't understand why I wasn't chosen to be part of the big clique.

One day, I convinced two friends to come sit with me in the South Lounge with everyone else. We managed to find three empty seats in the crowded, noisy cafeteria and sat down. My friends and I tried to relax, but I could read in their eyes that they felt foolish and uncomfortable. No one spoke to us.

At one point I saw one girl nearby mouth to the girl next to me, "Why are they here?" The girl next to me shrugged her shoulders and rolled her eyes, and the first girl started laughing.

This really upset me because both of these girls had been good friends of mine when we were young. I had never done anything to make them stop liking me.

After that, I gave up trying to join the group.

Eventually, I was able to ignore the preppies, and my friends and I made our own space separate from them. I guess I realized that if they didn't need me, I didn't need them. I didn't even like a lot of them that much. I had my own friends.

By sophomore year, my group had expanded to include about 30 people from all grades, known as the "pitters." A pitter was someone who hung out in "the pit," an area by the parking lot behind the school, next to some trees.

It was called the pit because it was the lowest point on the school grounds. But it was also a reference to our status in the school.

The pit was a place to get away from all the preps and others who thought we were no good. It was the only place where we felt in control. The preps took over the lounge, the parking lots, and the school in general. But no preppies came out to the pit.

The fact that the pit kids began smoking a lot earlier than the preppies gave us an image as the "bad kids." This label wasn't true, but it stuck to us all through high school.

I WAS CONSIDERED ONE OF THE STRANGE KIDS.

Though we resented being labeled, we also liked our image. We liked the power of knowing someone was scared of us. We felt that the preps had been stepping on us for so long; it was time for them to feel small by being scared of us for a change.

I hung out with the "bad kids" in the pit, but I didn't smoke. I was an honors student and I was respected by my teachers. I was proud to be a pitter, though, and I think my presence there helped to reverse some of the stereotypes that pitters are the kind of people who don't get anywhere in life.

And the preps weren't so perfect, either. Many cheated on tests and started smoking. Junior year, rumors began to fly about their wild parties. They would drink heavily and get high on the weekends, and their parties were hook-up fests.

The strange thing was, they seemed proud of that, because they'd talk loudly in class about their sexual exploits. I heard banter like, "Hey Doug, do you remember when we slept together sophomore year to get experience?" Or the head cheerleader saying to her friend in the middle of class, "Yeah, it was Alex's first time, so the sex was kind of lame, you know?" I guess having sex was a status symbol to them.

But they were still seen by everyone in town and in school as the good kids, the golden children, the kids who could do no wrong, even though they did.

The parents of kids who've done school shootings get a lot of criticism because they didn't know their kids were so troubled. But in my town, too, all the parents turned a blind eye to their kids' behavior.

So did the teachers and the police, who would smile proudly at the good kids while the pitters were considered lowlifes.

I'm not trying to say that all the preppies were bad people. But the preps' behavior was offensive to me because they were always seen as perfect students, athletes, and kids—when they were not. And we were seen as the bad kids, the outcasts.

In truth, we formed our own clique only because we were rejected by everyone else. The preppies pushed us aside. This hypocrisy still makes me angry.

THE LABEL WASN'T TRUE, BUT IT STUCK TO US.

I think school shootings could happen at any high school. But I don't believe the trouble is with groups like mine. I don't think it's the outcasts who are to blame. We should be thinking about the attitudes of the mainstream kids—the "jocks" or the "preps" or whomever—the popular groups in school who make other students feel rejected, angry, and depressed about themselves.

My group wasn't dangerous at all. We were just kids pushed aside who stopped trying to fit in.

The potentially dangerous kids are ones who withdraw from everyone, who seem hostile toward everyone. My high school had a group like this. A few boys didn't fit in anywhere. They wore dark clothes (really—it's not a stereotype) and sat in the back of their classes.

They weren't interested in school and didn't talk much to other people, but when they did they were rude to pretty much everybody. They loved computers, guns, and video games.

I can easily see how someone from that group could commit hate crimes. I can also see how it would be just like a video game for them.

Those boys didn't handle their feelings of alienation in a healthy way. The scary thing is that it's hard to tell the innocent, quiet, withdrawn kids from the hateful, planning, withdrawn kids.

The kids who do school shootings are not the only people to blame. I am not trying to justify violence in any way and school shootings are a horrible thing. But a lot of the kids who do shootings had been treated terribly. Even so, they will always be seen as the bad guys, the monsters. But isn't there another side to the story?

People need to understand how cruel the popular cliques can be to outsiders. The popular kids (and their parents) believe they're so perfect that they can't see their own faults.

Instead of pulling schools and communities together, cliques drive people apart. The popular kids become scared of the people they cast out, we all become more separated, and the alienation grows.

Andrea Uva *was 18 when she wrote this story. She later attended Occidental College.*

THiNk ABOUT iT

〉 Does Andrea's description of her school remind you of how students relate to each other in your school? In what ways?

〉 Why do you think students form cliques and separate themselves from each other? What could be done to prevent that?

A STRANGER IN A STRANGE SCHOOL

By Esther Rajavelu

I was really nervous about my first day of eighth grade, not just because I was a new student, but because I was also a new immigrant to the United States.

As I looked around at the other students in my school, I felt like I was the only person who was "normal."

I saw a skinny boy with pale skin, light blond hair cut close to his scalp, and the bluest eyes I had ever seen. I thought he was the weirdest-looking person alive.

Then I glanced at a girl with long black hair like my own, but her skin was lighter and yellower than my dark brown complexion. I noticed her eyes. They were tiny, black, and at first I thought she was squinting. I had no idea that people could look like that. I thought that everyone would look like me.

Finally, the teacher came and opened the classroom. I stood outside the door uncertain whether to go in and sit with all those weird kids, or to turn around and run home as fast as my feet would carry me. Then I remembered what my dad had told me that morning: "You have to study as hard as you can, actually even more. That's the only way you'll ever be successful."

I knew I couldn't study very hard if I didn't even enter the class, so I took my first steps towards my education in the United States.

I didn't know where to sit, so I stood looking for a friendly face. When I didn't find one, I just walked straight to the last seat in the last row.

As the teacher took attendance, I noticed two Indian names being called. I craned my neck to see where they were sitting and caught a glimpse of their backs. Nothing made me happier than knowing that there were people in my class as "normal" as me. I looked forward to getting to know them. I thought we would be great friends, because we were all from India.

The teacher gave everyone a program card. When she was finished, she said, "Go to your next class."

Everybody got up and walked out. I looked at my card. There were some codes and numbers printed on it, but I didn't know what they stood for. I sat in my seat wondering what to do next. When I saw some new kids come into the room, I got really worried.

Another teacher walked in, and ordered everyone to take a seat. He finished taking attendance and said, "Is there anyone whose name I haven't called?"

He hadn't called my name, but by now I was scared out of my wits. I knew I didn't belong in this class, and if I called attention to myself by answering his question all the kids in the class would start laughing.

Now I felt that I was the "weird" one and everyone else in the room was "normal." After all, they knew what was going on, but I had no hint about what to do.

I decided to pretend that everything was all right and sit as still as possible. Unfortunately, the teacher noticed me and said, "Hey, you in the last seat, did I call your name?"

I wanted to lie, but when I opened my mouth I said, "No."

"What's your name?" he asked.

"Esther," I said.

"Your last name?" he asked.

"Rajavelu."

"How do you spell it?"

"R-A-J-A-V-E-L-U," I said.

By now, all the kids had turned around and were staring at me. I was so embarrassed. All the confident feelings I had when I left my house were gone.

The teacher searched the sheet he had in his hand. "I don't see your name here," he said.

I already knew he wouldn't see my name, but I didn't know what to say. He asked for my program card.

THEY LOOKED AT ME AND LAUGHED.

"You don't belong in this class," he said.

I knew that too. I looked down at my hands.

"You have to go to room 410," he said. "You better hurry before the teacher marks you absent."

Without any warning I started crying. At first the teacher looked shocked, but then asked in a kinder tone, "Are you new to this school?"

"Yes," I mumbled.

He told me to take my bag and go to room 410 and he gave me a note explaining why I was late. I walked to the door with tears running down my cheeks, while the whole class stared.

At the door, I turned around and asked in a shaky voice, "How do you get to room 410?"

Matter of factly, the teacher turned to a boy in the front row. "Will you take this young lady to her class?" he asked him.

I followed the boy, who was short with a red face (I'll call him "William"). I thought it was so nice of him to walk me to class. As we walked down the hall, I wanted to let him know he was the only friend I had in the whole school. I was just about to open my mouth, when another boy waved to him.

William pointed to me and said something to his friend. I couldn't understand because it sounded different than the English I knew. They looked at me and laughed. I swallowed my thanks and stifled a new set of tears.

Finally, William left me at my new class, and I went in. I was so nervous. I would have given anything to go back home. I wanted to be safe with people I knew, not be stuck here with all these strangers.

I showed the new teacher the note and he asked me to come in.

"Sit down," he said, pointing to an empty seat in the middle of the room. I noticed that the Indian girl from my homeroom was sitting next to me.

She smiled. She was the first person to smile at me that day. I was relieved that she was sitting right next to me.

After class, we talked and I found out that we had most of our classes together. During lunch she took me to the cafeteria. We got our lunch and walked to a table where her friends sat.

"This is Esther," said my new friend. "She's new to this school."

They smiled and said hello and started asking me questions.

"Where did you go to school before?" asked another Indian girl.

"I went to school in India."

"Wow, so you just got here," said a white girl with braces.

"Yes."

"So how come you know English?" asked a Chinese girl.

I didn't understand what knowing English had to do with coming from India. I had spoken English since I was a little kid.

"My parents taught me," I said, just to be polite.

"You have a British accent," said another girl sitting at the far end of the table (at the time, I didn't speak like an American). "Have you ever been to England?"

I thought it was odd for her to say that I had an accent. After all, they were the ones who sounded strange.

"No, I've never been to England," I said.

Then they all started talking about their teachers, classes, the "school nerds," and all the cute guys in eighth grade. It was both the same and different from a conversation I would have had with friends in India. In India we spoke about teachers, classes, and "smart kids." But we never talked about guys.

This group was friendlier than I had expected and I began to feel at ease. I started the day thinking all these kids looked so strange and there I was eating my lunch, hoping they would be my friends.

On the first day I walked into school, my mind was filled with prejudices about my "normalcy" and their "weirdness." After five years of going to school in America, I now feel that "normal" comes very close to "weird," because who's to say what's normal and what's weird?

On that first day in school, if I could have seen myself the way I am now—with short skirts, eyeliner, and dark lipstick—I would have thought I was weird too.

Esther Rajavelu *was 17 when she wrote this story. She later attended Wesleyan University.*

THiNk ABOUT iT

|||▶ Have you ever felt, like Esther, that everyone else was "normal" and you were the "weird" one? What made you feel that way? Did anyone reach out to make you feel more comfortable?

|||▶ In your school, how are "normal" and "weird" defined? Are these labels fair? How do you define "normal" and "weird"?

Afraid to Learn

By Omar Morales

All my life I've been something of a loner and a sensitive kid. While other kids went out all the time, I was home listening to music, watching television, or just hanging out in front of the building where I live.

But my experience in school made me feel even more alone and made it hard for me to get an education.

Partly, I was just unhappy. But another part of it was that, freshman year, I started getting picked on. In class, one kid would always ask me a question about what the teacher had just said.

I'd answer back, "I don't know."

Then right away he'd start saying, "Damn, you don't know nothing, you're so dumb."

Things like that would happen a lot. Whatever people said would get to me.

For the most part, I thought my school was safe. It had a reputation for being one of the better schools. But in the middle of my freshman year I got a taste of how bad things were going to get.

Before Christmas vacation, I'd had an argument with a kid on the bus. Afterward, I didn't think that much about it. But when we returned from break, he attacked me from behind and pummeled me while I was on the ground. I missed two weeks of school because of the bruises inflicted on my face.

After it happened, my mom and I went to the police station and filed a report, but he didn't get arrested. I told the dean of my high school and showed him who did it to me. But he didn't get suspended.

A couple days after I returned to school, I saw him again on the bus and he was laughing and bragging about beating me up.

After that, I would sit in class and think about what happened a lot. Since some other kids in the school were still talking about the

> I HAD TO MAKE SURE I DIDN'T STARE AT ANYONE OR ELSE HE MIGHT TAKE IT AS A CHALLENGE.

fight, I couldn't get it off my mind. I felt humiliated and I felt an anger that I couldn't let go of.

And after that, I just couldn't focus. It's not that I didn't want to learn. I just couldn't get my mind to concentrate.

I'd had trouble concentrating in school before. I'd been held back because I had difficulties learning. But being in my high school didn't help.

In my sophomore year, some kids began wearing beads and joining gangs or just forming into groups. Every once in a while I would see one of my friends hanging outside near the school and he'd act like he wanted to ignore me. I figured he didn't want to talk to anyone who was not as tough as he was.

Inside the school, fistfights would sometimes break out. Outside, gangs and smaller groups would walk around looking for someone to rob, intimidate, or beat up. They would look for anyone who seemed weak and they would hurt them for fun.

Then they would laugh as they walked away, bragging about what they'd done.

Sometimes a bunch of kids would surround one kid and ask him, "Yo, you got some money?" and he would give them what he had.

One time I was sitting on the bus and across the highway I saw at least 15 guys attacking this one Russian kid. I didn't see the whole thing because the bus was already moving. But as I sat there I imagined how scared that kid must have been. He probably knew what they were going to do to him but didn't know how to stop them.

Every time I was outside the school I had to make sure I didn't stare at anyone or else he might take it as a challenge. And when I left school I had to make sure that nobody was following me.

This one kid at my school was pressured to rob. Earlier in high school he hadn't been a troublemaker, he was more of a joker. We'd see each other in the Resource Room, where we went to get help on our weak subjects.

He would crack jokes about the resource teacher and I would crack up. Then I would make a comment about her and we'd keep cracking up laughing.

But in sophomore year, some kids from his neighborhood were always trying to convince him to rob somebody after school.

Even though I knew he wasn't the type, twice I saw him hustle some guys for change. He didn't threaten anyone, and it seemed like he didn't really want to do it. I think he just couldn't say no, especially to his friends.

I think the reason people in my school were acting this way was because they wanted respect. They were probably angry because they didn't get respect anywhere, like in their homes or in their neighborhoods. They probably wanted to show people they were not to be messed with.

But I felt it was wrong to hurt other people for no reason. When I saw kids getting beat up, I sympathized with them because I knew how they felt when they went home, bruised and humiliated. The more threatened I felt outside my school, the more alone I felt.

By the end of my junior year, the safety around the school did improve. I guess most of the really violent students were either placed in another school, kicked out, or they just dropped out. We had gone through a couple of principals and the school was getting tougher on suspending people as soon as they got into a fight.

Now when I go to school I see police outside a lot more of the time. Things seem safer.

Right now I have an internship, so I don't attend school on a regular basis. And I'm glad that in January I'll be graduating. I'm tired of high school and the people in it.

My mother always used to tell me that you can't get a decent job without a high school diploma. She explained how hard it was for her because she dropped out her freshman year. So I never really thought of dropping out and I'm glad I didn't. Next year I plan to get a full-time or part-time job and I want to go to college. Eventually I'd like to work in a music studio.

Sometimes I think it would have been better if I had been more aggressive and just knocked someone after he said one word to me. But then I realize that wouldn't have solved anything.

I may have thought I was weak compared to the tough guys, but there was one good thing about being quiet and a loner. I didn't feel pressured to do things I knew were wrong. I didn't have to prove anything to anyone, like the kid from my school who started robbing.

In some ways I had to be strong in order to not follow what everyone else was doing.

Omar Morales was 19 when he wrote this story. He later attended community college and majored in business.

THiNk ABOUT iT

▶ After Omar is beaten by a peer at school, he tells the police and the dean of his school. But the other kid doesn't get punished. Have adults ever failed in protecting you? How do such failures affect the way you think or act at school?

▶ Omar says kids pick on each other in school because they want respect. Do you agree or disagree? What does respect mean to you? What are some better ways of getting it?

▶ What strengths does Omar show in dealing with his situation?

STICKING WITH YOUR "OWN KIND"

By Cassandra Thadal

Here's a scene from a typical day in my high school classroom: students from various countries, such as Mexico, Poland, Bangladesh, Yemen, and the Dominican Republic, are talking and laughing as they work together and help each other.

The teacher yells, "Why am I hearing you talking? Shouldn't you be working?"

"We work and talk at the same time," we answer.

When the clock marks lunchtime, we rush out of our classroom and head for the cafeteria. But by the time we reach our destination, the kids who mixed happily in the classroom have left that spirit of unity behind.

At most of the tables in the cafeteria, you see faces of the same color. The students enjoy this time with their own folks. The kids say they do this because it's just more comfortable. So whoever arrives in the cafeteria first gets her food and spots some seats, then saves a place for others of her same race or ethnic group.

After lunch, they leave together and spend the rest of the period in the hallways, or outside if it's not cold. A group of Polish kids settles on the floor near the main office, chatting and gossiping. Sometimes other Polish kids play checkers or dice nearby.

Some of the Dominicans sit in the hallway a few feet from the Polish kids. Most of the time they talk loudly and sing in Spanish or dance. A little further along, some kids from Ecuador or Peru hang out. The Bengalis gather in one classroom, listening to Bengali music.

The Haitian girls—the group I am part of—hang out next to our counselor's office, while the Haitian boys assemble on the stairs.

The students are allowed to roam around freely like this because my school is very small and generally there's harmony. People may have their personal disagreements, but groups rarely fight. That doesn't mean that everybody's friends, though—they aren't.

Of course, some teens do befriend people from different races. One Polish girl often hangs with a Filipina girl, and there are two black guys, one from France, the other from Africa, who are friends with a kid from Mexico.

I am also someone who doesn't stick only to her own race— although this wasn't always the case. When I first arrived here I had never spent any time with white people.

I lived in Haiti until I was 14. When I saw white people in Haiti, I hated them because I knew that whites had enslaved and mistreated blacks. I didn't know any whites who considered blacks their equals.

Also, some Haitians said, "Oh, the whites are so smart!" whenever they saw great things like computers or cars, as if no black person could invent things, and I hated that.

When I moved to the United States, I began to experience being around people of other races. I sat in a classroom and saw all different kinds of people. I wanted to talk to them—except the whites. My friends were Chinese, Honduran, and Haitian.

But when I saw the white kids, I said to myself, "I am not going to talk to these people." I assumed they were saying the same thing because I'm black. But gradually my attitude changed.

The white kids at school treated me nicely, and I saw that many blacks were doing great at my school. It seemed like in the United States, whether you were black or white, you could do great things. In class I learned that we all had things in common and I began to feel comfortable. My friends and I often discussed racism. We thought that teenagers should mix. Our culture and skin color differed, but we ignored our differences in the classroom and got along very well.

So it surprised me that when I returned to school last fall, I stopped mingling with other races and stayed with two Haitian girls. It didn't happen that way because I was being a racist, or at least I didn't think so.

It was because my Honduran friend, Daysa, was not yet back from vacation, and most of my old Chinese friends were in other classes. So every day during lunch, I started sitting with the Haitian girls.

After Daysa came back, I still spent most of my time with the Haitians. Daysa spoke with her friends in Spanish and I spoke Haitian Creole with my friends. I didn't see any problem with this until one day I got to the lunchroom before my two Haitian friends.

A friend of mine from the Dominican Republic asked me to sit with her, so I did. When my Haitian friends came, they looked at me strangely, but I didn't react and just said, "Hi." Then I ate my lunch and talked to the Dominican girl.

Later, when my Haitian friends were leaving, they passed and said, "Oh, yeah, Cassandra, you're buying the Spanish face." ("Buying someone's face" is a Haitian expression. It means that you ignore your own race and stay with another one because you think that the other race is superior, even if that race is disrespectful to you.)

MY FRIENDS AND I OFTEN DISCUSSED RACISM.

I laughed and said, "What do you mean I'm buying the Spanish face? Sitting with someone Spanish has nothing to do with that." Later I talked with one of my friends and told her that what they said wasn't fair and didn't make me happy.

"Okay, girl," she said, and that was it. We were again at peace.

I didn't take these things too seriously. They sounded more like jokes to me. But soon I realized they were not jokes. Later in the year, I became friends with a Russian girl named Natasha. We were in the same group in class and she was very nice to me. We always talked to each other in class and she often called me on the

I DIDN'T WANT MY HAITIAN FRIENDS TO TEASE ME.

telephone, but we never sat together at lunch.

One day my Haitian friends were sitting at our table while I was still standing in line. After I got my meal I saw Natasha and she called to me.

"Come sit with me!"

"Oh . . . I'm sorry. I have to sit with the Haitians or else they will say that I'm buying your face. You know . . . "

"What?" Natasha said, confused. I explained the expression and she said, "Okay, I'll see you later."

I left her by herself and went to my other friends. Because I didn't want my Haitian friends to tease me, I stopped hanging out with people of other races.

Sometimes in the morning I still walked around with one of the Chinese guys who had been my friend since ninth grade. My friends from Haiti never said anything about that, but another Haitian girl told me, "Cassandra, you love the Chinese too much. You're buying their faces."

I laughed and told her she was wrong. Still, I kept my friendship with kids from other races inside the classroom, because I hated what my Haitian friends said whenever I hung out with them at lunch.

The Haitian students mean a lot to me and I always try to get along with them because they're my people. I never told them how much I was bothered by what they said. Then I started to write this story, and I began to think about how we were all acting.

I realized I had become a different person by not mixing with other students when I wanted to. And when I realized that, I decided to change back to who I really am.

Now, in the cafeteria, I sit with Natasha, my Russian friend, along with my Honduran friend, Daysa.

I had stopped mixing with other kids because I was scared of what my friends would think and say. It's good to stay with "your people" sometimes. But, at the same time, if you only stay with your people, you're missing out on a lot of opportunities to make new friends and have new experiences.

We need to break down the walls of language, culture, and skin color if we want racism to stop. We share many common things, but the only way we can find out what they are is if we mix.

Cassandra Thadal *was 15 when she wrote this story.*

THiNk ABOUT iT

‖▸ In your school, do kids of different races, nationalities, or backgrounds mix together or stay separated?

‖▸ Why do you think kids sometimes prefer to "stick to their own kind"?

‖▸ Is it a problem when kids stay separated like this? Why or why not?

WHICH CrOWD DID YOU PICK?

By Satra Wasserman

Remember the first day of school, looking at all the kids, saying to yourself, "Who am I going to hang with?" Which crowd did you pick?

If your school is like the one I used to go to, you can probably draw a map of the lunchroom or of the sidewalk out front, with different colored areas to indicate all the different cliques and where they hang out.

On one corner are the jocks. Over yonder is the hip-hop crowd. Across the street are the nerds.

Then you have the rich kids with their latest fashions, the not-so-rich kids on their skateboards. And the list goes on and on.

I realize that at many schools the list wouldn't be this long, but at my high school it was.

In the first few months of my freshman year, I was down with the basketball team. I knew the whole squad. We would play basketball in gym class, we'd all sweat the same girls, and we'd talk about how funny looking our classmates were.

From September until springtime it was all good. Then JV basketball team tryouts came around and I didn't show up. These guys couldn't believe it. "Yo Sat, where were you?" they asked.

I told them basketball was cool, but that handball was my new game. It only took about one day for the reality of this to sink in with my friends. "Satra, you're playing handball with those weird kids?" they asked in disbelief. Then I was exiled.

Before, we would chill with each other all the time. Then, almost overnight, if I saw the guys from the basketball team in the hallway, they would act like we didn't know each other. Two years went by before I talked with any of them again. This is just one example of what happens with cliques.

Satra Wasserman *was 17 when he wrote this story.*

THiNk ABOUT iT

▐▶ Why did Satra's basketball friends "exile" him?

▐▶ What are the cliques in your school? Can you describe what they wear, what music they listen to, or other things about them?

▐▶ Can you draw a map of where they hang out in or around your school?

FASHION UN-CONSCIOUS

By Nadishia Forbes

Back home in Jamaica, I never really worried about whether my clothes matched. At school, the only thing that used to matter was how clean my uniform was and whether it was ironed. When I went to visit my friends, I would just put on a couple of freshly washed pieces of clothing without even thinking about how they looked.

We were kids—our friendships were not based on appearance. We just liked to run around and have fun. It didn't matter if our braided hair was pointing in all directions and our blouses and skirts had some buttons missing, or if we were barefoot and covered in red dirt.

I never experienced being judged because of the way I dressed—until I came to the United States. The first time it happened was on my first day of junior high school, which was also my first day in an American school.

I was a little scared that day, mainly because of the new environment. Walking down the hallway, I felt very self-conscious, so I turned around to get a better look at my classmates.

Two girls were staring at me, whispering and giggling. I stopped and waited for them to pass, but they said to go ahead, so I did. They continued looking at me, but I didn't say anything because I didn't know how to respond.

Even though I couldn't hear their conversation, I figured out it had something to do with the way I was dressed.

They were wearing expensive blue jeans and blouses, the latest name-brand sneakers, and their outfits matched. Plus, they had their hair permed.

I was wearing a pink and black plaid jumper with two straps in front, a blue, red and white striped long-sleeved blouse, thick black stockings, and brown shoes. And I just had big braids in my hair, because my grandmother didn't want me to perm it and that was fine with me.

When I got to my first period class, a couple or more of my classmates pointed out my shoes or clothes to their friends and laughed. Some of them even started throwing papers in my direction.

I looked different from everyone else and that was a big problem. When you start junior high, the pressure to fit in and gain respect is intense. The kids who made fun of me were popular—partly because their designer clothes made them seem cool. My clothes made me stand out and gave the others an excuse to pick on me.

I was the perfect target and it wasn't just because of the way I dressed. I was in a new environment and that made me feel scared and insecure. I was like a fish outside its water bowl. My classmates saw that I was in a position of weakness and wouldn't stand up for myself. They took advantage of that.

Almost every day, I would be greeted with giggles, pointing, and other demonstrations of their disapproval. For a long time, I didn't have any friends to back me up and the teacher did nothing to control the students. I felt like everyone was against me, like no one was on my side. Two girls named Luvia and Nefertiti were the main sources of my torment. They would put "kick me" signs on my back, throw papers at me, and make fun of my clothes.

For the first time in my life, I didn't want to go to school. When I got home each day, I would cry and complain to my grandmother about what was happening, but she was too busy to do anything about it.

Sometimes she would say, "Ignore them," or tell me to tell their mothers. Then she would force me to go back to school. She never really understood how hurt and depressed I was.

I would go to school each day with my heart pounding. I hardly paid attention and I never really learned anything. It was hard to concentrate on my schoolwork. The other students were very disruptive. Because I was quiet, the teacher always pointed me out as an example to the rest of the class. That made things worse for me

because I was now consid-
ered the teacher's pet.

FOR THE FIRST TIME IN MY LIFE, I DIDN'T WANT TO GO TO SCHOOL.

To take my mind off the fact that I might end up in a fight any minute, I'd bring a thick romance novel to school and just sit in class and read all day. Instead of focusing on learning like I should have, I focused on surviving by losing myself in books.

I did make one friend that year. Her name was Tina. She was really friendly and we had a couple of things in common.

We were both from Jamaica, but Tina had been here for five years. We both had strict families. Tina wore the latest styles of name-brand clothing, just like Luvia and Nefertiti, but unlike them, she never judged me because of the way I dressed.

Tina would defend me when the others were picking on me. She would tell them to leave me alone and always tried to help me out. One time, Luvia tried to spite Tina by saying that Tina and I were sisters. Later that day, I wrote a poem to Tina, titled "You're Like a Sister," and she liked it.

Having Tina as a friend made the days more bearable because I was not entirely alone. But it didn't make much of a difference in terms of how I was treated by the other kids. In fact, it didn't make any difference at all.

Around the middle of the school term, I started to think that maybe if I dressed like the rest of them, they wouldn't bother me so much. I hadn't made any effort to fit in sooner because I was stubborn. But I was tired of having people treat me like I was beneath them.

One day, I went to school wearing yellow socks and a yellow blouse with a black skirt. Right at the beginning of class, Nefertiti showed Luvia my socks and said, "What are you doing?" with a smirk. It was as if she were saying, "No matter what you do, you won't look as good as we do." Not knowing what to say, I turned my back, feeling a little defeated. I went back to wearing my usual outfits.

A month or two later, my uncle's girlfriend gave me a pair of name-brand sneakers. I wore them to school and I have to admit they gave me a little confidence. I thought I would get acceptance with my new shoes.

When I got to school, one kid actually announced to the class that I had on a name-brand sneaker and everyone looked. But I didn't feel any more accepted by my peers than I had before.

No matter what I did, they wouldn't let up. Luvia, in particular, was always throwing things at me or hitting me. I never started anything with her. She was always coming after me. Then the kids she hung around with would tell her how bad she was.

One day in the spring she was in the hallway, surrounded by her friends, when I passed by. When she saw me, she hit me. I didn't want to fight, so I started to walk by as I usually did. But, for some reason that day, I couldn't take it anymore. I decided it had to stop.

So when I saw Luvia in the cafeteria, I went up to her and slapped her face. The next thing I knew, I was on the floor. Luvia was much bigger than I, so it wasn't much of a surprise when I lost the fight.

Later that day, Luvia and her friends came up to me. She was very upset and kept staring at me, but she didn't say anything. I went home early.

That night, I told my father how these two girls had been giving me a hard time. He decided to take a day off from work and come to school with me and make a complaint. We went to the counselor's office. She called in Luvia, sat the two of us down, and asked about what was going on between us. Then she talked to us for a while.

I didn't really hear what the counselor was saying. I was too busy staring at Luvia and wondering what she thought about all this and what the other kids would think when they heard about it. After my father left, I went back to class. Everyone was looking at me.

After that, Luvia didn't bother me or throw things at me any-more, but she and her friends still gave me dirty looks.

When I finally finished seventh grade, I had the greatest summer of my life—simply because I had survived. I would stay home most of the time watching television, without anyone tormenting me.

In eighth grade, things got better. Everyone started to settle in and feel more comfortable. They let down some of their guard, which made for a less hostile environment.

My classmates stopped making fun of my clothes. I didn't really change the way I dressed, but I stopped wearing certain things—like skirts and dresses that made me look like I was going to church.

I got the chance to make new friends because everyone was friendlier. When I really got to know my classmates, I found out they weren't really bad people. And Luvia and Nefertiti weren't in any of my classes anymore, which made everything much easier for me. I didn't dread going to school.

That experience taught me never to judge people by appear-ance. I never tease anyone because of what they wear or how they look. I've also got the best of friends because I didn't pick them based on how they look, but by getting to know them as individuals.

Nadishia Forbes *was 17 when she wrote this story. She later enlisted in the U.S. Army.*

THiNk ABOUT iT

▣ Some of the adults in Nadishia's story—her teachers and grand-mother—don't understand what she is going through or are unable to help her. Other adults—her father and counselor—try to help but are unable to change things completely. What can adults do about teasing and bullying?

▣ Nadishia felt tremendous pressure to fit in with the other kids and gain respect. Have you felt that kind of pressure? How did you deal with it?

LIGHTEN UP ON HEAVY PEOPLE

By Jennifer Cuttino

There are many different types of prejudice—some people are prejudiced against skin color, race, nationality, religion, and appearance. I have been the victim of prejudice because I am overweight.

I am 18 years old and weigh over 200 pounds. I've had a weight problem most of my life.

Dealing with my weight problem in elementary school wasn't that hard. I wasn't teased too much because I was still young and I wasn't that heavy yet. But when I was in junior high, I was teased every day—mostly by people I knew. One boy named Taheed would say things like, "Hey, hey, hey, it's Fat Jennifer." He would laugh out loud and so would the rest of the class.

My weight was always the target of someone's joke. They would expect me to excuse them because they'd say, "You know I'm just playing with you." But I think that deep down they really meant it and didn't care about my feelings.

In high school I had the worst time. If there was a group of boys standing together when I walked in the halls, one of them would say, "Yo, there goes yours right there," or "Hey! My friend right here wants to talk to you." I would pretend to ignore them and just keep on walking, but deep down I was both hurt and embarrassed.

One day in my freshman year of high school, I got on the student elevator and went to the back. It was crowded and everyone was squeezed together. The doors wouldn't close and people started getting angry because they were late to class. Then someone yelled, "We're over capacity, throw all the fat ones out!"

At that moment everyone in the elevator turned around and looked at me. I felt like just curling up in that corner and dying.

Luckily the elevator doors closed and took us up to the top floor. When everyone got out, I had to force myself to go to class. I felt like crying.

Gym class was always a problem. I failed gym because I didn't want to get dressed or I didn't want to participate. I felt self-conscious seeing everyone else in their shorts or gym uniform while I was in my jogging pants.

Luckily, I've always had some good friends—friends who have stood behind me through everything. When someone teased me in school, my friend Kerri would always go up to him or her and defend me because she didn't like anyone bothering me. All of my friends have been on my side. They have accepted me for the person I am. They sometimes talk to me about doing something about my weight problem because they care about me and know how cruel and insensitive people can be.

Jennifer Cuttino *was 18 when she wrote this story.*

THiNk ABOUT iT

▶ Jennifer says there are many kinds of prejudice. What kinds of prejudice have you been the victim of? What kinds have you seen others suffer from?

▶ Have you ever been teased or harassed because of your appearance? How did that make you feel and how did it affect your life? Did it make you change your appearance, or try to change it?

▶ Do you have friends who support you, like Jennifer does?

LOSING MY FRIENDS TO WEED

By Jamel A. Salter

I had a lot of friends whom I grew up with, and growing up together made us very close—until my friends got too close to weed.

Before that happened, we were always together. We'd go to movies, parties, the park, and if we didn't have anywhere to go, we'd stay at one of our houses and play video games.

Even though we were close friends, we still had our little arguments. But when we argued, Dave would get in the middle and try to stop it. He was like the official peacemaker of the group.

Dave had the best sense of humor out of all of us. He was always telling jokes. That was one of the best things about hanging with those guys, you always got a good laugh.

But one day, when my friends and I were about 14, they made plans to put money in to buy some weed.

I didn't want to put any money in because I didn't want to have anything to do with weed. I thought if I didn't put any money in they would say I couldn't smoke and I would pretend I was disappointed. But they got enough money to go through with it and said I could smoke anyway.

Someone had to ride his bike 35 blocks to go get it. (The things people do for drugs!)

We were at the park when they started smoking it. One person lit the blunt, took a puff, and passed it around. I was in total shock because I had read and seen about drugs on television and here it was right in front of me.

As it was going around I was thinking to myself, "What should I do? Should I say yes or no?" I looked at how my friends were reacting after they smoked it. Since it was their first time, everyone coughed hard after they took a puff.

I sat at the end of the line, hoping that they would finish the blunt before it got to me or that someone else would turn it down so that I wouldn't be the only one who refused. Neither happened, and I found myself being handed the blunt.

"Chill yo, I don't want any."

"Take a puff son, it's mad nice."

"If you don't smoke, you're a herb."

"You can't be a mama's boy the rest of your life."

I got so tempted that I actually took it in my hand. But I knew that it was a choice between smoking and keeping their friendship or not smoking and keeping my health. I came to my senses and just passed it on.

"You really are a herb."

"You can't hang, mama's boy."

When they finished smoking, they started acting like fools. They were hitting each other and cracking stupid jokes. Seeing the way they acted made me glad that I didn't smoke. The next day everyone was talking about how bad they felt in the morning. You would think that would make them come to their senses and stop, but they just started making plans to get more.

BECAUSE I DON'T SMOKE WEED, THEY DIDN'T EVEN BOTHER TO CALL ME.

My friends have been smoking for a year now and it has changed them. They always look like zombies. Their eyes are always red and halfway closed. They have bad tempers and they are always ready to fight.

Especially Dave, now he has the baddest temper of them all.

A few weeks ago, we were at the park playing basketball. Dave had the ball and when I tried to steal it from him, I slapped his hand by accident. He got highly upset and started yelling at me.

"Why the hell are you fouling me?"

"It was an accident, and I don't know what you're getting mad about anyway," I told him. "It's all a part of the game. If you can't deal with it, don't play."

Dave tried to punch me but missed, then the others held him back and calmed him down. This surprised me because Dave was always the peacemaker before he began to smoke pot.

My friends and I always used to play against other kids in basketball, and I always started. I didn't hear about a game for a while but I didn't worry, because I figured my friends would tell me when they were playing. Then one day I called Dave to see what he was doing and his mother picked up.

"Hello, this is Jamel. Is Dave there?"

"No, he isn't, Jamel. He went to the park about a half-hour ago."

When I got to the park I saw them just finishing playing the other team. I got upset because I always started and now, because I don't smoke weed, they didn't even bother to call me. (By the way, they lost.)

Not being close to my friends like I used to be makes me think to myself, "Maybe I should smoke it just one time. What's the worst thing that could happen to me?"

Then I remember the way that they were acting that day in the park and I just forget about it.

You might be wondering why I don't stop trying to stay close to them and make new friends, but it isn't so easy to lose friends you've grown up with.

I keep trying to talk them out of smoking, because I don't want that stuff to make them sick. But they just laugh as if I'm stupid and tell me to mind my own business.

I wish our friendship could go back to the way it was before, but I don't think there's any chance of that happening while they keep smoking. I used to think that they were true friends, but now I know that it was just a game.

If not smoking is the reason why I've lost my friends, then I've been cheated. It's hard to believe that the difference between friends or no friends comes from one little blunt.

Jamel A. Salter *was 16 when he wrote this story.*

THiNk ABOUT iT

▶ Have you ever felt pressured to do something you thought was wrong? How did you deal with it?

▶ Jamel had to choose between having friends or staying away from drugs. What do you think of the decision he made? Why was it so hard for him to choose?

▶ Why do some kids want other kids to go along with what they're doing? Why is it hard for people to accept others who are different?

GETTING GUYS OFF MY BACK

By Artiqua Steed

My freshman year in high school was a difficult one, mostly because of my ex-boyfriend. Marcus would touch me in the hallways or make disgusting comments having to do with sex. Once during summer school he caught me in the staircase alone and tried to kiss me.

I hated him. Having to see his face every day was so unnerving. I felt really uncomfortable in school because of him.

Guys had said and done things like that to me on the streets, but I never expected to have to deal with that kind of behavior in my own school. I thought I was safe there. In fact, at the school's orientation, my parents and I were assured that it was a safe place. So why wasn't I safe from Marcus's obnoxious behavior?

I was angry but I did nothing about it. I couldn't go and tell on him because then I would be known as the school rat. I just gave Marcus dirty looks, hoping he would leave me alone.

What made it worse was that Marcus's friends started bothering me. After that, I couldn't even walk down the corridor without someone saying something totally perverted to me. One guy even came up to me and asked me if he could touch me. Did he actually believe that I would let him? I wanted to slap him for disrespecting me, but I didn't. He probably would have hit me back.

"Is it a curse?" I wondered. "Why is this happening to me? Why are guys so disgustingly stupid?"

I was being sexually harassed, but it took me a while to realize it, maybe because no one ever talks about it in school. Sure, they have sex education classes and even some parenting classes, but nothing is said about sexual harassment.

Not long after that, my friend Stephanie told me that when she was in junior high school, the guys used to harass her nonstop. Boys would grab her. One guy went as far as trapping her in the school bathroom where he tried to kiss her. Hearing her story made me understand what a serious problem sexual harassment is. I became determined not to let any guy harass me and get away with it ever again.

A couple of months ago, I was standing in the hall at school with my friend Derek. While I was talking to him, another guy, Jason, walked by me and touched my butt. Now, I've known Jason for two years and he was cool with me. But I couldn't believe what he had done. At first I was dumbfounded and couldn't say a word. Then I started yelling at him. He walked away laughing.

Derek was trying to calm me down. Then Jason came back towards me. I jumped at him and tried to slap him. I only touched a small part of his face because he had grabbed my arms when he saw what I was going to do.

I yelled, "Let me go!" and went to hit him again. Then Jason grabbed me and put me up against the wall. He didn't do it hard, it was just enough to pin me to the wall. When he let me go I was very, very upset. I could feel the heat rising off my face.

Derek didn't do anything while this was going on. I was mad at him for that. He told me that I was overreacting. I wanted to hit him too. But what would you expect from a guy? I don't think most guys understand how it feels to be sexually harassed.

I know that the way I handled it was not the best way. But I have to admit that it did make me feel better to hit Jason. I got my anger out.

I had to go back to class after that. Two minutes after I sat down, Jason walked in. When class was over I walked up to him and said, "You're in trouble." (Actually I said something else, but I can't write those words down.) Then I walked out of class.

Jason stormed out after me. He was like, "Why are you going to tell? Can't we just squash this? You did slap me." So I said to him, "Yes, I did slap you but not like I wanted to. And I slapped you because you touched me." Then he said something so stupid. He said, "Whatever you do, don't ever talk to me again. Just act like you don't know me!"

That made me even madder than I already was. Why would I want to talk to him after what he did to me? I started yelling at him all over again. One of the teachers heard and came out to ask me what happened.

After I told her, she told the co-director of my school. The next day a conference was held and I got to tell my story to the co-director.

They called Jason in and he denied everything that happened. Even so, the co-director believed me. Not because I'm a girl but because this boy was not a good liar. He couldn't have gotten his story straight even if he had taped it to his forehead.

First he said that he didn't even know me. Then he said that I just walked up to him and slapped him. The co-director asked him why I would slap him if I didn't know him. So then Jason said that we always play around in the hall like that. That made me want to hit him again, just for lying. But I controlled myself.

> I WAS BEING SEXUALLY HARASSED, BUT IT TOOK ME A WHILE TO REALIZE IT.

The next day the co-director came and commended me for speaking up about what happened and for not letting Jason get away with what he did. I don't know what happened to Jason because I was sent out of the room after I told my side of the story.

All I know is that I always see Jason in the halls and he is still in one of my classes. He has never bothered me again but he acts as if nothing has happened. He even asked me for a dollar the other day. I just looked at him like he was crazy.

I feel good about the fact that I didn't let Jason get away with harassing me. I'm also glad that my voice was heard. If something like that ever happens to me again I will do the same thing I did in this case (except I won't hit the person).

But I also think more should be done about sexual harassment in school. School shouldn't be a place where you feel uncomfortable. It should be a positive learning environment.

I think that schools should educate their students about what to do in these situations so they won't be scared to come forward. The schools should let students know that if they're harassed, they'll have people on their side, supporting them. That way more and more people will be encouraged to fight against sexual harassment in the schools. And the harassers will realize that they won't get away with it.

Artiqua Steed *was 16 when she wrote this story.*

THiNk ABOUT iT

⫸ Being sexually harassed makes Artiqua feel helpless and unsafe. Have you ever been in a vulnerable situation like that? Were you able to show the strength Artiqua did in dealing with it?

⫸ Artiqua says sexual harassment is a big problem in schools but no one ever talks about it. Do you agree or disagree?

⫸ At first Artiqua didn't want to speak up, because she was afraid of being the "school rat." Why are kids sometimes afraid to speak up about harassment or bullying?

MY BOY WANTED A BOYFRIEND

By Odé A. Manderson

One time, I was within earshot of a conversation between two older guys and one of them had a friend who revealed he was gay. The dude responded by saying, "I oughta kick your butt for telling me that crap. Get your gay butt outta here."

Even though I'm straight, it makes my stomach turn to hear comments like that. Why would someone go out of their way to hate on people because of how they live their lives? I think it's an exercise in stupidity. But I don't feel comfortable going up to strangers and calling them out.

Still, I admit that I have used the word *fag* when I wanted to insult someone's intelligence. No, I don't think gays are dumb, but it's a popular slang word. I know it's hypocritical and I'm trying to stop using the term, but old habits die hard.

And even though I don't consider myself to be homophobic, I used to think that gays act only one way because of how they're portrayed on TV and film. The actors who portray gays play it to the hilt with their bold sexual statements, style of dress, and comments about their gayness. Since I didn't usually run into anybody who acted in this way, I thought that gays would never cross my path, like they lived in a separate world.

I know now that I've probably been in contact with gays and didn't know it. In high school, my guidance counselor/college advisor mentioned in an offhand manner that he was gay during an assembly. I didn't think too much about it, though. I still didn't think that I would ever meet someone like me, but gay.

Then, during my stint working in a summer jobs program two years ago, I met Thomas. On my first day of work he introduced

> I STILL DIDN'T THINK THAT I WOULD ever MeeT someone Like Me, BUT GAY.

himself to me and quickly became a good friend.

He was different and cool. I learned a lot from him, like how to take action when times called for it and to speak my mind a lot more. He had a sense of humor, and he was straightforward about everything. Evidently, he found me equally cool to be around.

We eventually started to hang out on the weekends. Sometimes we chilled at the mall. Other times we would hang out at a diner after picking up our paychecks. Or we would go to his cousin's crib, where we watched cable or listened to music.

When we were hanging out, I picked up on some signs that made me think Thomas might be gay, like the feminine quality of his voice, and the way his hips swung back and forth when he walked.

I didn't want to jump to conclusions, which is why I never said anything about it. In reality, you can't tell someone's sexuality that easily. I felt that I couldn't assume Thomas was gay unless I heard it come straight from his mouth.

I didn't let it become a big issue with me. We were cool, so it didn't matter.

But toward the end of July, Thomas started to spend more time alone. He went from being outspoken to quiet, and I started to wonder what was going on. I came home from work one day, and was barely in the house for an hour when the phone rang. It was him.

"What the hell is the matter with you?" I demanded. "Dyin' or something?"

He started to say something smart, but stopped. He sighed, then put down the receiver. A few seconds later, someone picked it up.

"Hello?"

It was one of his cousins.

"Look," she started. "Thomas has something to say to you, but he's too shy to say it. Do you know what it is?"

I wasn't a total idiot. Or so I thought.

"Does it have anything to do with his sexual orientation?" I asked calmly.

"Yes, it does. That's not all, though. The reason why he had a hard time telling you was because he has a crush on you."

I was shocked. Butterflies suddenly fluttered in my gut, then turned into wild hornets, which felt like they were bursting through the wall of my stomach. Then a bright-colored spot appeared in front of my eyes. I was silent for a moment before I decided to say something. I was prepared to hear him tell me he was gay, not that he had it for me.

His cousin said that he liked me because of my looks and personality. I blinked hard.

"Tell him he has nothing to be shy about," I replied, trying to compose myself. "Put him on the phone."

I heard a faint "here" as she passed the receiver to Thomas.

"Yeah?"

"That's all you had to tell me? Look, you didn't have to tell me anything, so trusting me with that was strong of you. And this won't change our friendship, if that's what you're thinking. I'm cool."

Right after I hung up the phone with Thomas, I called my good friend Darnell because I needed some feedback and advice. The minute I explained what happened, he burst out laughing.

"Odé, that's the worst," he said in between snickers. "He's in love with you, baaaaaabeeeeeeeeee . . ." he added in a sing-song voice. "I would've screamed on him," he suddenly stated coldly.

"For what?" I said. "He knows where I stand, so it's not a problem. Plus, he's peoples."

"True, true," Darnell said. "I still would've screamed on him," he added.

But I didn't want Thomas to feel bad that he'd told me. After hearing how kids our age treat gays—the threats, the jokes, and the violence—he was probably scared that I'd go and wild out.

After that, we still hung out as before, even though we didn't talk about his sexual orientation or his crush on me again. I didn't want to bring anything up. I was thinking of how I would take it if I were gay and a straight friend started asking me about it. I thought that would make me feel uncomfortable. I didn't want to risk saying something stupid that would make Thomas feel uncomfortable.

I wanted to know if he was happy with himself, even though other people probably didn't accept him because he's gay. But I didn't ask. I didn't want to make him feel like he was on trial for being who he was. I also wondered if he still had a crush on me.

Knowing a guy had feelings for me was unsettling. When girls liked me, I felt a sense of satisfaction. But with Thomas, I felt bewildered. The idea of any guy liking me caught me off guard. This was a new experience and I felt uncomfortable.

At the summer job where we worked, a lot of the employees caught on to Thomas' feminine mannerisms.

"Is he gay?" female counselors would ask me. Since I hung out with him, they turned to me for info.

"Yo, is that guy gay or somethin'?" the male counselors would ask. Then, answering themselves aloud, they'd add, "Yeah, he's gay."

Because of attitudes like that, I think that gay teens are forced to live life differently than straight teens in many ways. They have to be careful what they say and do in front of other people. Most people only want to know if someone is gay so they can go in for the attack.

So I tried to be very respectful of who Thomas was, even though I wasn't perfect at it. And Thomas would sometimes bring up stuff on his sexuality. Those talks let me know where he was coming from.

One time we started discussing relationships, and we swapped stories. He said that he had been involved in long-term relationships. His boyfriends were usually four to five years older than he.

He would talk about how guys treated him and how he felt about the person he was dating, but he didn't go into too much detail. I didn't ask for more information because I didn't want to overstep my boundaries as a friend, and I think he knew that.

I THINK THAT GAY TEENS ARE FORCED TO LIVE LIFE DIFFERENTLY.

For the rest of August, we hung out as much as we used to before Thomas came out. The only time I felt uncomfortable was when I let my tongue slip sometimes, using *fag* near him.

I wanted to kick myself because I didn't know how Thomas took it. It didn't seem to bother him, and that really threw me off. It made me feel stupid, because I knew it was disrespectful.

I think he understood that when I used the term it wasn't directed at him being gay, but regardless, it is a term that makes fun of gays. I didn't want to seem insensitive to him.

After a little while, I stopped wondering if he still had a crush on me. It didn't matter. Even if he still had feelings for me, it wasn't changing our friendship.

But when the summer ended, we didn't keep in touch. A few weeks later, I began lifeguard training and went back to school and dated a few girls. He was trying to get a good job. We weren't able to chill as much because we had less time.

After school started, he called twice just to see how I was holding up and what I had been doing, but he didn't ask to hang out. Neither did I. I figured he just didn't want to hang out anymore. I don't know why.

Even though we're not friends anymore, I'm glad that Thomas had the guts to come out to me. I'm impressed that he kept it real and revealed who he was.

And I think our friendship showed me how my perceptions of gay people were pretty off. In reality, signs of gayness are nowhere near as cut and dried as they seem on TV, because gay people don't all act the same.

Thomas made me realize that gay people aren't so stereotypical and have things in common with straight people. Thomas had some of the stereotypes in the way he walked and talked, but he was also quiet and thoughtful. He wasn't loud at all. He couldn't even tell me about his sexuality himself.

I've realized I don't live in a separate world from gay people and I don't want to discriminate against them. Ten years from now a gay person could be my boss or my son's godfather. For all I know, my son could be gay. And I wouldn't love him any less.

Odé A. Manderson *was 17 when he wrote this story. He later attended college and majored in writing.*

THiNk ABOUT iT

‖▶   Thomas helped to break Odé's stereotypes about gay people. Has anyone helped you break stereotypes you had about a group of people? How did that person help you break them?

‖▶   After Thomas reveals he has a crush on Odé, Odé doesn't abandon him as a friend. How do you feel about the way Odé handled the situation? Have you ever been in a similar situation with a friend?

‖▶   Has anyone stereotyped you? In what ways? How did being stereotyped make you feel?

Princess Oreo Speaks Out

By Dwan Carter

"If I wasn't looking at chu, I'd have thought you was white."

"Say that again, you said that mad white."

"You're just weird."

I often get comments like that from classmates, friends, and even my family. Sometimes I laugh back, but the comments also hurt my feelings. I know they don't mean anything by it, but I don't really like that they think I'm so strange.

I'm a dark-skinned female, a descendent of Africans. I grew up in a black family in a largely black neighborhood, and I'm conscious of the disadvantages that have plagued African Americans for generations. So what's the deal?

It seems that, for a lot of people around me, being black is an attitude. According to my peers, if you're black, you listen to hip-hop, R & B, and reggae. The ability to dance is a given, and of course, you know how to do dances like the Bankhead Bounce and wining. You eat Caribbean foods and Southern-style cooking and, if you're female, you know about head wraps and weaves.

Anything beyond that and it's like you're from another planet, or at least that's how I feel. I do a lot of things that people around me don't associate with being black. My friends laugh at me because I don't like certain black rappers. They love to tease me about watching TV shows that have mostly white characters.

It doesn't seem to matter that I also watch TV shows with mostly black characters. Because of my tastes and the way I talk (I use big vocabulary words), people jokingly call me "Oreo": black on the outside, white on the inside.

But to me, being African American means my skin color shows a history of enslavement and discrimination. Knowing my history and understanding where I come from is very important to me. It's what keeps me grounded and focused on taking advantage of the opportunities that African Americans fought for.

My dad instilled that knowledge and pride in me. As African Americans, he says, we should be in debt to those who risked their lives to give us the opportunities we have, particularly education. His understanding of what it means to be black has a lot to do with our history and our future.

But for my peers, being black has more to do with fitting into the culture right here and now. They make me feel like I'm not black enough. And they tease me even more when I try to be (their version of) black.

THEY TEASE ME EVEN MORE WHEN I TRY TO BE (THEIR VERSION OF) BLACK.

When I try to be down with the slang and fit in, half the time I end up sounding like a fool.

"Ah-ight, peace yo."

"You's a Doga man."

"Peace out, boo-boo."

It just doesn't come out right. The words get all jumbled and tumble out wrong, and my friends look at me as if I've spoken to them in another language. All my efforts end in giggles (I'm laughing at myself right now) or in gut-busting laughter with tears streaming down my friends' faces.

My friends tease me even worse when I try to show them that I can dance to reggae, calypso, and hip-hop. It just doesn't work well. I'd never get invited to *Soul Train*, more like *Soul-less Train*.

It's not just friends who paint me "white." One time, my sister and I were reciting some lyrics from a rap song. My sister was reciting the lyrics and I was singing the hook. I was trying to be just like the female singer—the bounce in her movements, the way she moves her neck, her hand motions, everything.

I was so into the song, I forgot my sister was in the room with me. I thought I was doing well until my sister's hard laughter broke my concentration. She was doubled over with tears streaming out of her eyes. She was laughing so hard she couldn't talk, and her hand was motioning for me to stop.

Then through bits of dying laughter she said, "Stop . . . stop trying to act ghetto, girl, you making my sides hurt." She said I looked like a duck having seizures.

I didn't let it show, but it hurt that even my own sister didn't see me as black enough.

What bothers me about being called white—besides the fact that I'm not—is that it makes me feel like I'm lacking something, and I'm not sure what it is.

My friend told me once, "Maybe one day you'll wake up and become Dawnesha." At the time, I was a geeky freshman in high school, insecure about who I was. I wondered if I could transform myself into someone my peers would recognize as a true black girl.

I'd have loved to put on those big hoop earrings I saw my friends wearing. I'd be wearing snake-patterned denim outfits, popping my gum, and showing off a nameplate that said "Dawnesha." My hair would be dyed, fried, and laid to the side. And when I'd rank on somebody, I'd use those fluid motions of the neck and hand that make the "African-American girl" infamous.

Sigh. I would've loved it. I just wanted to fit in.

Then reality knocked some sense into me. I didn't have enough attitude to pull that off. And it just wasn't me.

Now, as I reach my final semester of my senior year, I'm more aware of myself, who I am, and who I want to be: me. Even saying "Dawnesha" makes me feel weird. That's not who I am. Dwan is my name and I'm comfortable with that. Being different makes me unique. I even gave myself a nickname, "Princess Oreo" (though my dad hates it).

I'm getting used to people staring at me when they hear me blasting rock music. I think it makes them feel uncomfortable because they're not used to an African-American girl bobbing her head along to rock and roll.

"Hey," I want to tell them, "music is music."

My reading tastes are diverse, too. I like to read books by white authors, such as Isaac Asimov and Tami Hoag, as well as by black authors, like Octavia Butler, Toni Morrison, and Malcolm X. Maybe it's because I read a lot that I talk the way I do.

It's not that I'm purposely acting white—it's not even a thought that crosses my mind. I just like what I like, and I don't know why other people can't be more open-minded.

Dwan Carter *was 17 when she wrote this story and later attended Spelman College.*

THiNk ABOUT iT

⫸ Because Dwan is black, people assume she should behave a certain way. Have people ever assumed you should behave a certain way because of your race, the way you look, or for any other reason? How did that make you feel?

⫸ Dwan tries to fit in by speaking slang, but it doesn't come out right because it isn't her. Have you ever tried to fit in with others by being someone you're not?

⫸ The "acting white" issue is really about peer pressure. How big a problem is peer pressure in your life? Is it ever possible to totally ignore it?

I'M BOTH ArAB AND AMericAN

By Rana Sino

Right after the September 11th attacks on the World Trade Center, my school decided to allow students to express their feelings about the tragedy. I understood that everyone was very upset about what had happened. I was upset too. But the teachers really should have had some consideration and asked if there were any Arab Americans amongst us who would rather leave the classroom than listen to the insults that followed.

Little did anyone know that the quiet student who was sitting by herself in the corner of the room happened to be an Arab and was listening to all of their insults, hatred, and anger. See, there was no way they could guess that I'm Arab, because I dress very American, I have light skin and blonde hair, not to mention that I talk with a New York accent.

For the first few minutes, the students were just screaming and cursing about how the United States should "bomb every one of those $%^&#$." Then some students said that every Arab should die, and called them smelly, dirty, and so on and so forth.

In my school, the teachers believe in letting students speak their minds. So as the students were raving on, all my teacher did was tell them to keep their voices down and watch their language.

I sat quietly and acted calm. Inside, I felt a flame of anger that kept growing with every disgusting word that those kids were saying. Still, I felt so bad about what had happened, that I just told myself that everybody had a right to be angry.

I stayed quiet until one kid said that he had never thought about joining the army, but now he couldn't wait to enlist, get a gun, and blow the heads off of every person he sees who even looks Arab.

That's when I lost my tolerance and screamed, "Why wait for your diploma? Why don't you just shoot me now?!"

Everyone suddenly quieted down and looked at me as if something was growing out of my head. I was glad I screamed. I couldn't take hearing that hatred anymore.

I have many Arab friends and they all feel the same way I do. Actually, most of them feel worse. They have been harassed because they look more Middle Eastern than I do. My friends and I have gotten abuse even from people we know. Some people from my neighborhood have called my brother and me "Bin Laden and his sister," or "terrorist twins," or "ugly A-rabs." Those words hurt, although they're not nearly as bad as getting beat up or even killed!

The thing that really gets me is that even though I was born in Saudi Arabia, I have spent almost my whole life here and I love the United States, maybe more than a lot of people who were born here and don't really understand how lucky they are to have the freedoms and comforts we do.

One reason I don't want to leave is because in this country I have learned to be an independent woman. In too many Middle Eastern countries, women have to stay home, take care of the children, and cook and clean. My father thinks in this very traditional manner. He thinks girls and women should look up to, honor, and respect their fathers and husbands, sort of like gods.

That attitude drove me crazy when I was living with him and was one of the reasons I went into foster care. But at least in this country, I know that I am much more than a piece of property. I am allowed to go to school, get a good job, have as many or as few children as I want, and even make more money than my husband! And I get to pick that husband too (that is, if I want one), without having to worry about my father choosing a husband for me.

I also love the education that I've gotten in this country. (Despite the harsh words I heard from some students, I especially love the school I'm in now.) I love the fact that there are so many opportunities.

Then there are the smaller things I love, such as the music and going to rock concerts. I love the opportunity to eat Chinese food, Italian food, Indian food, and fast food all in the same day! I love the way the buildings look, and especially the fact that I would never have met my dear boyfriend, who is Hispanic American, if I had stayed in Lebanon, where my family lived after moving from Saudi Arabia.

Most important, I love that I have the freedom to say no to things I don't want to do, or say, or take, or anything!

I COULDN'T TAKE HEARING THAT HATRED ANYMORE.

I love this country for all those reasons and more, so when people attack me for being one of "them," they don't know a thing about how I feel. And they don't know what it means to be an Arab, either. I have always been proud to be Arab.

Just like I love America, there are also things that make me feel connected to the land that I'm originally from. For instance, I like listening to Arab tunes every now and then. (When I go over to my mother's, she has lots of tapes.) And as much as I like the mosh pits at a rock concert, I still like to belly dance to Lebanese music (when nobody is looking). I like Lebanese food like grape leaves and stuffed vegetables and chickpeas and stewed beef. Most importantly, I feel a strong connection to Lebanon because most of my family is still there. I believe I can love America and still be proud of being Arab.

Seeing Arab Americans become the target of people's anger after September 11th has hurt, but I'm still proud to be an Arab American. It's just that now, I have to be a little more careful about who knows it. I wish other people in this country would direct their anger at Osama Bin Laden and whoever else proves to be responsible for the loss of so many innocent lives. They shouldn't make victims of more innocent people.

Rana Sino was 18 when she wrote this story.

THiNk ABOUT iT

▶ Have you ever blamed a group of people or felt anger toward them because of what a few members of that group did? Do you still feel that way? Why or why not?

▶ Have you ever been attacked or blamed because of the actions of a group you belonged to? For example, you may have heard people putting down all teenagers. Or you may have heard people putting down your racial or ethnic group. How did you feel? Did you speak up, like Rana?

GAY ON THE BLOCK

By Jeremiah Spears

Because I'm 6'6" and hefty, people often think I should be a ball-player of some sort. But once you get to know me, you'll know I'm no ballplayer.

In my old neighborhood, guys would always call me out of my house to play basketball, knowing that was not what I liked to do. When I missed a shot they would ridicule me and call me a faggot.

It's true, I'm gay, and though I look like your ordinary clean-cut boy, I act a little feminine. When I'm happy, I like to buy shoes. I also like to read romances and family-oriented books. My favorite book is *Mama* by Terry McMillan. It's about a divorced black woman with five kids who's having problems being accepted into society.

In fact, I've been different my whole life. I first realized I was homosexual at an early age, because when I was around 5 or 6 years old, I would see boys and think, "How cute." Besides, I was labeled as different by many people. I never liked to play ball or get sweaty. My favorite toy was Christmastime Barbie. When the boys used to roughhouse and try to get me to do it too, I'd tell them to leave me alone. I would never do anything that boys did, such as sports, play fighting, or singing to rap music.

I could never understand why anyone would want to harass me for that. I used to think, "So what if I'm gay? So what if I'm different? Accept me or don't accept me at all, honey, because I'm just me." I couldn't understand why the boys wanted to bother me and fight me when they didn't know a damn thing about me. But they did.

The boys in my neighborhood were rough-necked, ball-playing, weed-smoking boys who picked on people to prove their toughness to their friends. I think those boys did what they did because of their own insecurities, because they wanted to prove they were manly men. There were about nine or 10 of them and they lived in or around my neighborhood. Wherever I went I always ran into them, and often they would torture me for being gay.

One Halloween night, I went alone to catch the bus to go to a party. I was wearing a pair of dark jeans and a matching jacket and a black sweater with my initials on it. My mother had spent a lot for the outfit. She had spent $132 on the jacket alone.

While I was walking toward the bus, I saw a group of boys on bikes passing by. I recognized some of the guys. The first thought I had was, "Oh no, they're going to start trouble with me." I kept walking.

All of a sudden a bottle of urine hit me and got all over me. Some straight guys think doing something like that to a gay guy is kind of creative. They all hurried away and I screamed and cried because of all the money my mom spent on the outfit.

> OFTEN THEY WOULD TORTURE ME FOR BEING GAY.

Then I felt the same as always—puzzled as to why I had to be their victim. I thought these guys would never understand me. I felt like the things the boys said and did to me were marks for life.

For three weeks after Halloween, I had the incident on my mind. At first my brothers wanted to beat the boys up. But I thought it wouldn't make the situation better. It would probably just wild up the problem more.

Finally, I decided that I'd show them I wouldn't stand for it anymore and I began to fight—with my pen. I wrote them gruesome letters smeared with ketchup for fake blood to let them know I was going to get them back and that I'd get the last laugh. Ha!

Usually, when the guys harassed me, I would tell them, "Go straight to hell because I'm going to be me and there will be no changes until I feel that my life needs a change." And I would get revenge. I would make fun of them trying to talk to girls and getting turned down. Then I would get physical with them.

When we fought, often my brothers or my girl friends would be there to help me—some of my girl friends were known for beating guys down. And once I even whacked a guy with a plank. While I was fighting, I'd think blood and more blood, because of the traumatic experiences I'd been through. I wanted so much revenge on the boys who created trouble for me. Because of the fights, the cops were always at my house.

Even though it made me feel better for a short while to get revenge, I felt as if I was never going to succeed in having peace of mind. And after the fights were all over, I wouldn't feel much better. Often I felt as if I never belonged, and that no one would ever socialize with me because I was gay. I thought the world was so against me and that no one cared.

Still, there were people around who helped me and supported me, like my brothers and my friends. Looking back, I can see how much of a difference they made, even when times were at their hardest.

When I was living in my old neighborhood, my best friend was Lauryne. We would go to the movies, the mall, or just hang in the park and talk about everything, from boys and love, to clothes, shoes, and jewelry.

Like a lot of my other girl friends, Lauryne didn't really care that I was gay. As a matter of fact, she praised me for having the nerve to be able to come out at an early age to my parents and siblings and not really worry what they were going to think of me. She said things like, "You're brave," "You're courageous," and that she was lucky to have a friend like me.

It made me feel wonderful to know I had friends who honestly cared about me. It made me strong and gave me courage to be even more open about my sexuality, and to encourage other kids to come into the light and take the risks. It made me believe there would always be people to support me.

Another person who really helped me survive everything was my grandma, who raised me. From my grandma I learned strength, courage, patience, love, heartfulness, and to treat all people the same no matter what. My grandma taught me to learn new things from people who try to reach out and teach you. She taught me the golden rule: Do unto others as you want others to do unto you.

My grandma was born in 1919. She grew up on a farm and was born in a time when blacks weren't accepted and women weren't allowed to vote. My grandma saw so much—the Great Depression, both World Wars, prohibition, segregation, lynchings, civil rights. She would tell me about the marches, about the violence, and how once when she was in Jackson, Mississippi, she saw men cutting down two boys who had been lynched from a tree. She would tell me that life isn't that hard today, not after what she's seen and been through. She told me, "My dear, you haven't seen the harshness life can give you."

Sometimes people who have lived through hard times grow closed and mean and bigoted against people who are different from them. But my grandma had a strong sense of herself, and that made her open-minded to the different things in life. She always said, "People must know themselves before they try to learn from another person," and that's exactly what she did.

My grandmother never tried to change me. Instead, she encouraged me to do what I thought was right and what would make me happy. My grandma often told me I would be different as time went on and that she'd always love me however I was.

Three months after I came into foster care, when I was no longer living with my grandma because she was ill, I received a call from my aunt saying my grandma wanted to speak to me. When she got on the phone, she said, "I love you dear, and don't let no one turn you around." Then my grandma hung up the phone because she had gotten short-winded. Shortly after that conversation, she died. I loved her dearly and I miss her.

I now live in a group home for gay and transgendered boys. As for the boys in my neighborhood, they no longer bother me because I don't go around there very often. When I think back on things, sometimes I can laugh, but other times I'm still angry that those nobodies had so much control over my life.

Still, I think I have come to be okay being myself every day. Despite all the hassles I went through, the people who supported me made me feel that I didn't have to change myself for anyone. My life would only get harder if I tried to change to satisfy other people. I just need to satisfy myself.

Jeremiah Spears *was 18 when he wrote this story. He now lives in Mississippi.*

THiNk ABOUT iT

▶ Why do you think some people pick on gays and lesbians?

▶ Jeremiah faces terrible abuse, but his grandmother and his friend Lauryne don't care that he's gay and stand by him. Is there someone in your life who has stood by and accepted you? What has that person said or done to make you feel accepted? Have you ever done the same for someone else?

NASTY GIRLS

By Alice Wong

At the end of eighth grade, my classmates and I hung around after school signing each other's yearbooks. After my classmate Diana signed mine, I noticed she'd written, "Thank you for getting me into the gossip group."

I was shocked. I felt horrible. I didn't want people to associate me with a group labeled "the gossip group."

But, the sad thing was, the girls in that gossipy group had been my closest friends for much of junior high. I don't know which I felt worse about—that I'd been part of their clique or that they'd kicked me out of it.

I met the members of my clique—Maggie, Marsha, Kayla, and Bethany—in sixth grade, the first year of junior high school. They were friendly and outgoing, and they helped me meet some new friends too—which I liked, since I was shy.

I was also naïve and thought everyone was kind. I thought my new friends were funny. They talked to me about their problems and I confided in them. They seemed to fill all the qualities I was looking for in friends.

My friends were also striving to be popular, and as the semester progressed, they got what they wanted. People in school knew who they were. For me, being part of the popular group was okay, but it wasn't as important as being accepted by a group.

But during that year, I also began to notice changes in their personalities. They seemed to think that being popular meant putting everyone else down.

Kayla was the leader of the group. People wouldn't know whether or not the rest of us agreed with what she said because we were robots. We went along with her even if our own opinions were different.

One day, Kayla pointed at an eighth grader in the hall and commented loudly on "what a big nose" he had. The group laughed, but I didn't. I thought it was rude.

Another time, Kayla kept pointing at some guy and laughing. I didn't see anything funny about him, but the rest of the clique did. They noticed his crooked teeth. They tended to notice all the little things about a person, things I didn't focus on when I saw someone.

They loved to label people "dorky" or "geeky." They gossiped about how people acted or what they'd heard about them through friends and acquaintances.

I often thought about what would happen if I told them how I felt when they were mean, but I was afraid to because I didn't want to lose their friendship. I was used to them and thought it would be too difficult to get to know a new group of people.

I was also afraid that if I spoke up, they'd all turn on me as well. I'd already had a taste of how it would feel to have their cruelty aimed at me.

One of the girls in the group, Bethany, had a particularly mean attitude and sometimes put me down like she did people outside our group. One day, I was wearing a name-brand shirt and she came over to check the label.

"Is that real?" she said in a very obnoxious and loud tone as she peered and tugged on the back of my shirt. Everyone just stared. My cheeks turned red from embarrassment.

She knew I wasn't the type who'd confront her, so she took advantage of my weakness. I felt hurt and angry that other members of the group did nothing to stick up for me.

I was beginning to really dislike my friends. But I still wanted to be part of their group.

When eighth grade began, I hung with the clique during lunch and before and after school, but I also started to make new friends. I met people like Eva and Melissa in different classes, and I could talk to them about things like our favorite bands and how we liked to sing and write poetry—things my old friends couldn't have cared less about.

Whenever I was with my new friends and saw the girls in my clique, it was awkward. I usually didn't introduce them to each other because I didn't think the girls in my clique would be interested in meeting them.

Then one day, about three months before eighth grade ended, I sat down at my clique's usual lunch table. The clique was late, so I waited for them alone. After a few minutes, they came. Marsha and Maggie said hi, but Bethany and Kayla said nothing.

I WAS ALSO AFRAID THAT IF I SPOKE UP, THEY'D ALL TURN ON ME AS WELL.

I didn't know why they were acting so distant toward me, but I thought if I just left it alone, they'd get over whatever was bothering them. So I went to where some of my other friends were sitting and chatted with them for a while.

When I came back to the clique's table, Kayla gave me this stare. I knew something was very wrong indeed. She said she had something to discuss with Marsha and didn't want me to listen to the conversation. I was like, "Okay," but felt left out.

I went to chat with my friend Jacqueline, who was sitting in the far corner of the lunchroom, but in the back of my mind I kept wondering what was up with the clique.

A few minutes later, the bell rang. On my way to the exit, Kayla called me over to the table. She told me that she didn't like that I associated with friends outside the clique. She said that if I wanted to remain in the group, I had to follow their rules. She didn't exactly say she wanted me out of the group, but it was obvious from her expression that she did.

The rest of the group just stared in silence at us. They already knew what she was going to say and do. Kayla snickered while she talked to me. She was having fun rejecting me.

I was shocked, and then, as her words sank in, it really started to hurt. For the rest of the day, I tried avoiding her. I felt like crying, but I didn't want to show her how badly her words hurt me.

When I got home, my mom saw how troubled I looked and asked, "What's wrong?"

"Not much. I just have a lot on my mind."

I didn't feel like talking. I was very upset. But Mom was persistent. I finally spilled my guts.

She said things would get better. She assured me that everyone has problems like these, and I should accept that that's just how those girls were and that I couldn't change them. The only person I could change was myself.

But even though I'd known for a long time that they were mean to others, I couldn't accept that they'd been so cruel to me. I already missed them, because I'd been a part of their group for so long.

For weeks, I didn't have much of a social life. I kept to myself during school. I didn't hang with anyone after school. I wasn't up to doing anything fun. I was too upset. All I wanted was to be alone and have time to think everything through.

I even lost my appetite. My mother prepared my favorite dishes, like barbecued spareribs and fried noodles, but I only ate small portions.

The way my friends turned on me made me feel like I couldn't trust anyone. I began analyzing everything the girls in the clique had said to me. I felt like I should've figured out how Kayla and Bethany were going to treat me before it was too late. I was scared that if I were open with my new friends, they'd wind up hurting me too.

But, noticing I was blue, my new friends emailed me jokes and poems to try to brighten my mood. At first, I was too upset to find the jokes funny. But after a few days, I reread their emails and they made me laugh.

One Saturday, Eva and Melissa dragged me out to the park to play basketball, twirl on the balance beams, and ride our bikes. Then we went out for lunch. I had so much fun. I began to realize who my true friends were.

Still, it wasn't until the end of the summer that I really started to feel better. Thankfully, making new friends wasn't that difficult.

I realized I should've left the old clique once I knew how they were instead of waiting until they forced me out. I'm glad I'm no longer part of that group. If I was, I might've become as closed-minded as they were and missed out on the opportunity to meet new people.

I still feel guilty for the years I was a friend to those girls. Even though I didn't do most of the mean things they did, I continued to be a part of their group.

I'm still cool with the other friends I made in eighth grade. And when I went to high school, I was relieved to find that most people were much more respectful toward each other than in my junior high.

I started associating with all sorts of people who were friendly and kind. I didn't care anymore if I fit into any one group.

Now I realize that being in a clique doesn't determine my worth. When I was in the clique, people in and out of the group saw me as naïve, and I was close-minded to new people. Now people see me as an outgoing, friendly, and kind person, which is a more accurate reflection of who I am and want to be.

Alice Wong was 17 when she wrote this story. She majored in journalism in college.

THiNk ABOUT iT

▶ Did you ever belong to a group that did things you didn't agree with? Did you speak up to the group about them? Why or why not?

▶ Is it hard to be popular and stick to your values at the same time? Why or why not?

▶ Are cliques always a bad thing? When are they a good thing?

STICKS AND STONES

By Yen Yam

I always thought being Chinese was a curse. When I was growing up, I lived in a mostly black neighborhood and I had friends, but I didn't fit in. At first, I didn't think too much about my race. Then, in first grade, two boys started calling me "small eyes" and making some karate noises. At first I didn't know what it meant. I was only 6 years old.

Much later, when I was watching a Bruce Lee movie and saw him making the same stupid kung fu noises, I finally realized that they were messing with me because I'm Asian. Their jokes were only the beginning. Growing up, I was constantly made fun of because of my name, my looks, the way I talk, everything.

Even my friends teased me. One girl would always say, "Yenny Yam, how about some egg rolls?" Another friend would say, "Chin chun chun," and then squint his eyes at me.

I know that sometimes they were only joking around, but it really hurt my feelings, even though I never said anything about it. I don't think my friends thought it was hurtful, but they knew it was embarrassing for me because my face would become red and they would laugh about it.

Most of my friends were black, and some never said anything racist to me and would defend me to others. But their help was not enough.

And the teasing wasn't the worst of it. One very clear and sunny day, my cousin Amy and I were taking the long way home from school, walking through the parking lot of a Baptist church. We saw these two black kids we knew from school, Damien and Shawn.

They yelled crude remarks at us, like, "Chin chun, egg rolls, Chun Lee," and some other mean words regarding our race. Amy yelled at them to shut up and go away. That was when they started to throw rocks at us. One rock hit me straight in the chest. It

> # PEOPLE WOULD HURT ME IF I SAID SOMETHING THEY DIDN'T LIKE.

hurt so much and I got a huge bruise.

I didn't tell anyone because I was a quiet and shy girl and I was always too scared to say anything. I think that made me an even bigger target. But Amy did tell her brother, and he went to talk to Damien's mother.

The next day, Shawn told me that he had a huge sister and she was going to beat me up if I got his friend in trouble again. I was scared. After that, I began to think that I was not a kid anymore. People would hurt me if I said something they didn't like.

I was not just teased by black people, but by white and Hispanic people too. When I was 8, these two white boys would throw rocks and sticks at us and call us names. But often I was most angry at my black peers, because it seemed like they should have known better.

I am not writing this to disrespect African Americans. But I would wonder why blacks were making racist remarks to me when they should have known better than anyone that it's not right. They should have thought of what their ancestors had been through—and their parents and grandparents, and themselves—and realized that they were doing the same thing.

When teachers would teach us about slavery, civil rights, and segregation in class, the black students would talk about how they are treated unfairly because of their skin color.

I used to sit in class and think they were talking a lot of junk. They would mess with me one minute and the next they would make an about-face. They would say crude things to my face, then preach that it's wrong to judge by skin color.

I don't think they realized they were being hypocritical. When people think "racism," they tend to think "black and white." But the way the people in my school acted toward me was racist, and getting treated like I was not even worth the dirt they stood on really hurt me. It made me angry. It also made me feel ashamed of being Asian.

I have never been sure whether to fight back or stay silent. I am afraid if I do say something back, it will just make people even more cruel.

One time I did speak my mind, and it only made things worse. I was working in my family's restaurant when a couple of guys started to say some perverted stuff about Asian girls. I got mad and started to argue with one guy. He ended up grabbing a container full of rice that we use as a paperweight and throwing it at my head. I ducked and it missed my head by inches.

I was scared, but I looked him in the eye, staring him down, trying to make it seem like I wasn't afraid of him. Inside, I wanted to cry.

I think I'm too small to fight back, but I wish I could. I think people tend to believe Asians are a weak race and are not able to stand up for themselves, so it makes me feel weak when I make that stereotype true.

But at least my brother Prince always stands up for himself. Once, when he and his friend were eating pizza, two teens started to call them names, wanting to start a fight. They were surprised when he and his friend fought back. I'm not a person who likes violence, but I was proud that my brother fought them, even if he did sprain his wrist.

Even worse than feeling angry is feeling ashamed of who I am. When I was younger, I used to wish I was a white girl with a white girl's name. I love their big, light eyes and light hair colors. Instead, I have plain, dark brown hair and small, dark brown eyes.

When I used to play house or hotel or school with my cousin, we would always become white and I would pretend my name was Elizabeth White. I also pretended that I was rich, because back then I thought all white people were rich.

I used to wish that I was able to change my name for real, because no one else had such a weird name—Yen Yam. I used to hate having my name called out because someone would always have a comment about it. It wasn't until I moved to New York and started high school that I met many people with unusual names. Before, I felt like I was standing out like a sore thumb.

You might think with all these angry feelings that I would become bitter and hateful toward others. But I don't treat people differently because of their skin color. I am a shy girl, and I get to know people before I have an opinion about them.

Besides, I've always known people who don't judge by skin color. I want to be like those people, not like the people who have hurt me.

I know racism really comes from ignorance. I even see that in my own family. When I was growing up they would sometimes say that black people are dirty or bad people. I would always say that there are dirty and bad Chinese people too. But it's hard to change old ways of thinking.

I think the way the older people in my family grew up has a lot to do with why they look down on other races. They grew up in China, where they knew only Chinese people. In the United States, they are unable to communicate with others. So they just think the worst, based on what they hear from their friends.

The people who were messing with me were similar, in a way, because they didn't know anything about Chinese people. They based their comments on what they had seen on television.

Right now, I don't know how I should feel, though. Should I still feel angry at the people who have done this to me? Should I get revenge? Should I feel sad? I don't know. I'm confused about everything.

But at least I don't feel like my heritage is a curse anymore. Over time, I've become more comfortable with who I am. But sometimes I still feel lost and alone. Sometimes I wonder, "Where do I belong?"

I was born in the United States and don't speak much Chinese. So here I am different because of my skin color. In China, I would be regarded as an idiot, an outsider, because I do not understand the language.

Sometimes I feel like an alien who doesn't fit anywhere in this world. It's strange to belong to no country and to feel like you have no people of your own.

Yen Yam *was 18 when she wrote this story. She attended college and majored in economics.*

THiNk ABOUT iT

▶ Have you ever felt "cursed" because of the racial or ethnic group you belong to? Why did you feel that way? Did the feeling eventually change?

▶ Yen says that racism comes from ignorance. Do you agree? Where do you think it comes from?

▶ Do you agree with Yen that the African Americans who teased her should have known better? Why do you think people who are discriminated against can discriminate against others?

BEATING THE BULLIES

By Miguel Ayala

I've had an anger problem for a long time. It has included crying, yelling, cursing, screaming, and intimidating people. When I was at my worst, I would turn violent and destroy property and throw things. I even tried to kill myself.

The reason I have an anger problem is plain and simple. I grew up in a violent home. My mother would slap, whip, and beat me and my siblings. Also, she would torment us with words that to this day still hurt me. She would call us terrible names if one of us dyed our hair or for messing up on paperwork she was supposed to do. She would beat us for the smallest things, like making noise, playing too rough in the house, or accidentally breaking things. She'd beat us until we bled or had welts all over our bodies.

That wasn't the only side of her. Sometimes she would laugh with us, take us on family outings, nurture us, and really show a mother's love. Those times I really loved her. All this love and hate mixed together made me very confused and angry. Sometimes I took the anger out on myself, sometimes on other people.

When I was 12 my mother gave me $7.50 for a class trip, and instead I bought a video game magazine. She found out and whipped me with an extension cord.

That night I felt so much anger, I didn't know what to do with it. So I contemplated horrible things. I thought of sneaking out of the apartment, going to my roof, saying a prayer, and then jumping off.

In the end, I made it through that night without hurting myself. But the worst of my anger was yet to come.

Back then, I never released my rage on my mother. I was afraid that if I did she might beat me to the point where I'd be disabled or even kill me. So instead, I took my rage out on other people, usually at school. I would fight and steal. Many times I would curse at people in public and say obscene things to females. I was a terrible bully.

It made me feel a little better to do those things. It made me feel like I had all the guts in the world, and making other people feel as mad as I felt released my rage. The only problem was that those people would always want to whip my butt for it. And sometimes they did.

Then one day I really lost it. It was a beautiful, warm day. I was 14 or 15. I lost a music cassette tape. At first that didn't bother me. Then I started imagining that my mother and brother had taken it just to get me mad. Thinking this way made me angry. I started yelling at my brother and my mom. Then I really went crazy. I was crying, and before I knew it, I'd gone to the china cabinet in the kitchen and rammed my elbow into the glass cover. I cut myself pretty bad. That's when my family sent me to the hospital.

The doctor who bandaged my cut asked me a bunch of questions to see why I did it. But I brushed them off and said I just lost my temper. They thought of sending me to a residential treatment center where I could get more help with my anger, but my mother wouldn't sign the papers to let me go. Looking back, it might have been a good thing for me to go to a residential treatment center where I would have been away from home and might have gotten a lot of adult attention and more mental health services. Instead, I kept living with my mother's abuse and feeling angry.

I did go to a special school because of my behavioral problems. There I had therapy and group meetings three times a week for almost two years. They were trying to get me to work on my problems: Fights, Acting Out, Acting on Impulse, and, my personal favorite, Self-Destructive Behaviors, like when I tried to sharpen my finger in a metal pencil sharpener.

The school was good for me because it gave me a support network of adults who cared. I had all these people who wanted to help me with my problems. It felt like winning the lottery.

Eventually, I began to open up to those people. I told one of them that I was contemplating suicide. Telling someone that made me feel a little less alone. But when I started talking with a psychiatrist, I realized I could lose my regular life and go into foster care if I kept telling my secrets, so I tried to just think happy thoughts and act like I didn't have any real problems.

But my anger and thoughts of suicide didn't go away.

One day my brother was cursing a girl on the street, and I thought he was cursing me. So when he came upstairs, I started to curse him out. My mom started to yell at me and sent me to my room. I went to my room and slammed the door. My mom came in my room with a golf club and started to beat me with it. I lost my marbles. I started to yell, curse, and cause a tantrum, so the police were called. They thought I was suicidal, so they brought me to the emergency room. Then my mom said, "I don't want him no more." So I was placed in my first group home.

It was a good idea for me to be removed from my mother, but I hated being in a group home. (Still do.) I was so scared and pissed at the same time. But I also hoped that finally I might get help with my anger problem. It was always getting me into fights. Instead, my anger seemed to get worse.

> # THE reASON I HAVE AN ANGer ProBLeM IS PLAIN AND SIMPLe.

There were so many things in group home life that triggered my anger—the bickering, the teasing, the stealing, and the fighting. When I would have a problem with a resident and staff would intervene, I would curse and stuff like that. Then, when I really needed help from staff, the words I'd said earlier would backfire and they wouldn't help me. I got moved to a lot of different group homes because of my anger.

After a while, I started thinking about suicide again. I just couldn't find a way out of my sadness and I did not trust anyone enough to talk about my feelings. The sadness was not just connected with my abuse. It was also because of life in the group home. I didn't feel very safe there.

I even had a plan: I would either jump off the roof of my mother's building or jump in front of a subway train. Then one day I made a spontaneous attempt on my life. It was April Fool's Day. That day, a lot of things had gone wrong. My favorite staff member was arrested due to a false allegation. I got into a fight with a friend of mine and he and his brother jumped me. I took out my frustrations on myself. I cut myself with a piece of glass.

Soon I was in the hospital. I thought I would be in there forever because of what I'd done to myself.

While I was there, I began to think about a lot of different things that had happened to me. I thought about all the abuse I'd endured in my home and at all the group homes I'd ever lived in. It wasn't the pain that bothered me, it was the fact that I would always find myself in the same situation over and over again. It seemed that people were always hitting me—my mom, my foster peers, sometimes even group home staff. I'd wonder if this pattern would ever stop. What if I got married? Would I face abuse from my spouse? Would I be abused by my kids? Could I break the cycle and try not to be around people who would abuse me? Did I and my anger cause people to abuse me?

There was one patient in the hospital who was old and he couldn't talk or defend himself. He could only grunt. I didn't want to be like him. I didn't want to have the same old problems forever and end up defenseless in a hospital.

So I said to myself, "I don't care what it takes. I am going to succeed! I am going to prove to all those who hurt me in my life that I have a future!" I thought maybe I'd want to try to help more people like myself so they would not suffer what I've suffered. To do that, I needed to live.

After my discharge from the hospital, I was motivated to change my life. I started to go back to school. I did my chores and cleaned my room and showed a decent amount of respect to the staff. I started yet another program for my anger. This one paired me with a therapist who was on call 24/7 (via beeper).

Not all those changes stuck. I stopped going to the program after about a month. I don't always do my chores anymore, and I still get into fights. I still struggle with my anger, and sometimes when I think about my past, I just want to die. My anger still gets me moved around a lot, and recently I've been going AWOL pretty frequently. But I do feel a little more motivated to not really slip up since I tried to kill myself. I guess that showed me how serious my anger is, and I feel determined to not let that happen again.

Still, I don't know what needs to happen for me to get a firm grip on my anger and emotions. I've been in a lot of programs, and not all of them have had much of an influence on me or my anger. I think the ones that helped the most were the ones where I had a good relationship with the staff there.

I guess anger is the kind of thing that takes a long time to deal with. For now, I try to focus on the positives in my life and I try not to think about my problems too much. When that doesn't work, I tell myself that if I give in to the stupidity and really lose it, then I'm letting the bullies win.

Miguel Ayala *was 19 when he wrote this story.*

THiNk ABOUT iT

‣ In what ways did Miguel's mother abuse him? Which is worse, emotional abuse or physical abuse? Why?

‣ Because Miguel was abused by his family, he takes out his anger on others. Do you think most kids who bully other kids were mistreated themselves? Why or why not?

‣ Miguel realizes that suicide is not a solution to his problems. What do you think can help him take care of his problems?

IT AIN'T EASY BEING HARD

By Danny Ticali

When I was younger, I used to think being bad was cool. I was very insecure and all those guys who were hard or tough seemed so strong and confident.

The media also began influencing what I thought I should be. I used to watch TV shows or movies that had lots of violence in them. I'd also listen to songs that would talk about beating or killing people. I wanted to be tough like that.

I can remember sitting on street corners with my so-called "homeboys" drinking beer and waiting for some trouble. All we did was sit and talk about how crazy we were and how many people we could beat up.

My memory from that time is pretty dazed, thanks to marijuana and alcohol. But I remember brief moments of fights, and other things I did that today I'm not that proud of.

I had a big problem with who I was. I was very angry inside. I had a lot of my own problems and I was confused. My family and I wouldn't talk that much. And when we did, they would tell me to be a certain way—a nice preppy boy with short hair who always dug his nose into the books.

Meanwhile, television and music were telling me the opposite. They made me think that the average kid was a tough guy. I thought that to be normal you had to be hard. I thought you had to hurt people and fight and hang out with the bad boys.

So I tried to be like everyone else. I tried to be hard and a hood. I wanted everyone to admire me for how strong I was, and how confident I was. I did some bad things, like steal from a few stores, and beat people down 'cause I didn't like the way they looked.

I remember one time I ran into this kid Johnny, whom I didn't get along with. When I saw him, me and my friends began to stare at him. So he and his friend yelled, "What are you looking at?"

When we heard Johnny loud mouthing us, we ran across the street yelling, "Who do you think you're talking to?" and began to beat him and his friend down.

> **I HAD A BIG PROBLEM WITH WHO I WAS.**

I was upset afterwards, because I wasn't mad at him, I was just pissed off in general. So I went out of my way to hurt him bad just because he asked me what I was looking at!

Those kids were afraid of me and that didn't make me feel good. I felt ashamed, because I hardly knew them and they felt they had reason to fear me. When people were nice to me or gave me things, I felt it was because they feared me, not because they liked me.

Slowly, I began to realize that acting that way didn't make me feel better, it made me feel worse. I felt like I was hiding and lying, so I began searching for myself.

It was a slow process. When I got dressed in the morning, I'd ask myself, "What would I like to wear?" not "What would my friends like?" People began to notice the changes in me, but I no longer cared what other people thought.

One day I saw a couple of people who I knew were about to jump another kid from the neighborhood. I just happened to be walking by when they started fighting with him.

Because I knew the kid and I thought he was a nice guy, I jumped in and took his back. When everyone saw that the neighborhood bad guy—me—was involved, they wanted to chill.

After that day, I began to carry myself differently. I gave people the benefit of the doubt before I passed judgment on them. And I gave 110 percent for my friends 'cause they always returned it. The kid whose back I took in that fight is still my friend to this day.

Nowadays when I read the paper and see all the violent crimes that are being committed, it makes me think how lucky I am that I'm not dead or in prison by now. Maybe I would be if I hadn't decided to change when I did. And there are so many others out there who are like I was when I was younger—not really bad, just in need of a little direction.

I've seen too many of my friends screw up their lives or die because of stupid stuff. I'm sure that some of you out there know how I feel. We've got to put a stop to this. We've got to keep our noses clean and our heads clear. We've got to stay away from the garbage.

I've learned that we don't prove how tough we are by beating people up. We do it by being able to say no and think for ourselves, by being able to take it when some people start making fun of us. We have to give a damn about our lives and our futures, and let that guide our actions.

Danny Ticali *was 17 when he wrote this story. He majored in human services in college.*

THiNk ABOUT iT

▕▐▶ Danny says that TV and movies made him feel he had to be tough and violent. Do TV and movies cause people to act violent? What, in your opinion, makes people violent?

▕▐▶ What do you think being tough means? Is it important to you to be tough?

AT HOMe IN THe ProJecTS

By Fabiola Duvalsaint

The projects. A year ago I would have shuddered at the thought of visiting one and being around the people who live there.

Like most people, I didn't know anything about public housing projects because I had never been to one. But that didn't stop me from imagining what they were like.

To me, the projects were a place where dangerous people lived, a place you didn't go if you didn't live there. I mean, people in the housing projects are mostly drug dealers and prostitutes, right? Basically, they were forbidden territory.

My neighborhood wasn't the kind with white picket fences up and down the block. For a while, my neighborhood was thought of as dangerous. But I believed my neighborhood could change for the better. I didn't think that about the projects. I thought they were made for tough people who weren't to be messed with.

The way they made projects look on TV, how could you not be scared? The tall buildings that all look the same, the drug dealers racing to see who can make the quickest sale, and the daily shootings.

If a girl in school passed by with "door knocker" earrings, baggy pants with the boxers hanging out, and a bandanna wrapped around her head, one of my friends would look at her and automatically say, "Here comes the projects." And everyone at our table would burst out laughing.

Then I met Maria. We met freshman year in gym class, but we weren't really friends. Maria was tall, Hispanic, had wild, curly black hair most girls would die for, and was very blunt.

If she didn't like something, she would let you know it in a second. She spoke her mind and didn't care about the consequences.

The following year we had a math class together. One day, I noticed she had a cool blue nail polish, so I asked for the name.

She looked at me as if I was stupid and said, "It's blue." After that I was like, "Forget that!"

Then one day a girl dropped her pen in class. When she tried to get it with her foot, she got stuck. Maria and I started laughing. We were laughing so hard that the whole class was watching us. After that, we just started talking like two friends who knew each other from way back.

For a while during junior year we got separated. But one day we bumped into each other and decided to meet at a fast food place once a month after school.

Then once a month turned into once a week and, before I knew it, Maria and I were getting together every day, either to hang out at my house or at the school's athletic field.

One day I asked if I could come over to her house.

"You want to come over my house?" she asked, looking like I was talking in a foreign language.

"Yeah," I said. "What's the matter?"

Maria just looked at me and smiled. "I live in the projects," she said.

I looked to see if she was kidding, but deep inside I knew she was dead serious. How was I going to get myself out of this situation?

I guess she could tell how I felt by looking at my face, because Maria told me right away that I didn't have to go if I didn't want to.

I wanted to back out, I really did, but I sensed that not going would mean my friendship with her wasn't real.

When my last class ended that day, I went to meet Maria at our usual spot (the locker room).

As we started to walk, Maria looked at me and started laughing. I asked her what was so funny (because at this point I sure needed a good laugh).

"You're scared to go to the projects!" she said.

I turned toward her and looked her straight in the face. "I'm not scared. Why should I be?"

WAS THIS WHAT I WAS AFRAID OF?

Great! Not only was I a coward, but I'd turned into a liar too.

I wanted to turn back, and had almost decided to, but just then Maria pointed to an orange building surrounded by other orange buildings.

"Here it is," she said.

I had been so filled with dread and my thoughts were so locked on turning back, that I didn't even realize that we had already arrived.

When I looked around I was shocked. There were no drug dealers on the corners and I certainly didn't hear any gunshots. This neighborhood was quiet and calm—as if all the people who lived here were sleeping inside their apartments. Was this what I was afraid of?

We crossed the street and went inside her building. When we got upstairs to her apartment, I met her mom and sister.

I got so comfortable in her apartment that my fears melted away. My worries were all just gone!

Her apartment was like any other and her room was just as messy as mine, which made me even more comfortable.

She had a dog named Rufus that went wild when he saw me, and a quiet cat that just sat around. Her mom looked harmless.

When it was time to leave, I told her that this time I really wasn't scared and I could manage to get to the bus stop across the street on my own. After that day I went over to Maria's house often.

Now I've grown to learn the true meaning of the saying, "Believe none of what you hear and half of what you see." And I am not as ignorant as I used to be.

Fabiola Duvalsaint *was 17 when she wrote this story. She majored in journalism in college.*

THiNk ABOUT iT

||▶ Did you ever have a fear of a person, a group of people, or a place based on a stereotype or prejudice? Did you get over that fear? Why or why not?

||▶ Has anyone ever been mistrustful or afraid of you? Why were they afraid and how did that make you feel?

MY SECRET LOVE

Anonymous

I was born and raised in a rough neighborhood, where I learned to walk and talk tough. I know who to watch out for on the street, like dudes who carry liquor bottles and wear too much red. (There are a lot of gang members around my way.)

The way I dress reflects my neighborhood, so most people expect my taste in music to follow the same pattern. Mean streets + Pelle Pelle jeans + cornrows + Timberlands = hard-core rap 24/7.

That's partially true, because hip-hop is a major part of my life. But there's also a hidden part of me. It's not something I like to talk about, even if you paid me. If I did, people would laugh long and loud. It's not easy for me to admit this, but . . .

I love musicals.

Yep. *The Sound of Music, The King and I, Carousel, West Side Story* . . . you name it, I've seen and enjoyed it.

I like the emotions given off by musicals, the way the story and the songs blend together to make a single presentation filled with dancing and catchy show tunes. I like watching Mary Poppins fly around with an umbrella, singing about medicine going down nicely if you take sugar with it.

But you're not listening. You're too busy laughing at me. The way I began this story, you probably thought I had a drug problem. If I did, I would have gladly put my name on this article. No one would laugh at me if I was addicted to cocaine.

Musicals and I go way back. *The Sound of Music* was the first one I saw, back in sixth grade. My teacher rolled the TV into the room, switched the lights off, and let the show begin. I sighed and braced myself for what I thought would be the whackest class of my 11 years.

But then, when the characters started singing, it suddenly became interesting to me. Characters would be talking about something, then they would just jump into song. As I watched the film, I realized I was being introduced to a revolutionary concept— a full-length movie that conveyed emotions through music and singing.

In one of the most memorable scenes, the main character, Maria (played by Julie Andrews), comforts the kids she is taking care of. The children are scared of a raging storm, so she begins to sing about her "favorite things" to take their minds off their fear.

A few weeks after the viewing, the entire school had to do renditions of various musical numbers on stage in the auditorium. My class had to sing "Sixteen Going on Seventeen" from *The Sound of Music*. One part was sung by the girls and the other part by the fellas. We did well, and my self-confidence never faltered during the performance.

> NO ONE WOULD LAUGH AT ME IF I WAS ADDICTED TO COCAINE.

But after my performance in sixth grade, I lost interest. My attention span was really short when it came to new things. Musicals were the last thing on my mind until my senior year of high school.

My music teacher rekindled my interest. He showed flicks like *Carousel* and *West Side Story* to our class every week as examples of different kinds of music. The other kids didn't appreciate it at all, but every day I secretly hoped he'd continue showing them.

My music teacher was gay and white, so admitting that he liked musicals didn't hurt his reputation at all. I, on the other hand, wouldn't be able to take the "oh yeah, he's gay too" stares I knew I would get if people knew my secret.

But one day, I took a chance and admitted to some friends at work that I had watched a few musicals.

"Come on, sing a show tune you know," someone said.

"Yeah, don't be shy."

"Why not?" I said after a moment's hesitation.

I attempted to repeat my stellar sixth grade performance in response to the earnest requests of my co-workers. So I started singing that still familiar song in a mock soprano voice.

"I am 16, going on 17, I know that I'm naïve . . . fellows I meet may tell me I'm sweet, and willingly I beleeeeive . . ."

(Okay, so for some strange reason, I only remembered the girl's part.)

Instead of applause for my attempt to bestow culture upon them, what followed was 10 minutes of uncontrollable laughter. And mocking.

Ingrates.

But really, what's so bad about liking musicals? The music is catchy and you have visuals. They're similar to the modern music video, but they differ because videos focus mainly on money, drugs, sex, or violence in its rawest form. A lot of these topics are watered down in most musicals because they were made in the beginning and middle of the 20th century, when things were less explicit.

But today's teens can still relate to many of the messages that musicals convey. For instance, in West Side Story, Officer Krupke pisses off the Jets gang royally. They want to go out and release their anger violently, which would've sent them straight to the slammer.

Instead, they perform a dance and song, "Cool," which helps them control themselves and avoid getting arrested. It was similar to Michael Jackson's "Beat It" video in terms of attitude and how they would lash out unexpectedly with a "Pow!" or "Bam!"

Even though musicals and music videos have many similarities, kids my age who come from the block would probably never allow themselves to appreciate show tunes unless they're being sampled by rappers. The dudes in my neighborhood and high school are all about rap and R & B. They'd rather listen to rhymes in Japanese than take in alternative styles.

There's a black kid I know who listens to rock bands all the time. But he doesn't tell anyone. Because he fears being ridiculed by his peers, he expresses his love for alternative music only to his closest friends. Like him, I'm afraid to come out of my creative closet because I want to avoid being mocked.

But it's still unfair. Just because I'm a rough dude who happens to like watching films where people abruptly break into song and dance shouldn't automatically draw people to the conclusion that I'm a freak.

I don't want to be the butt of jokes or to be looked at as pitiful. I don't want people to say, "My life is messed up, but I'm better than the cat who likes musicals."

I just don't get it. Why can't I sing songs from *The King and I* in peace?

The writer was 17 when he wrote this story. He later attended college.

THiNk ABOUT iT

- Is there something about yourself you hide, because your peers wouldn't accept it? What is it, why wouldn't they accept it, and how does it feel to hide it?

- Have you ever judged or teased someone because of his or her tastes in music, clothes, or something else? How do you feel about that now?

MY GROUP HOME SCAPEGOAT

By Angela Rutman

"That's why your mother left you in McDonald's with a Happy Meal, you stupid fool."

"At least I have a mother."

"Who's your father, Ronald McDonald?"

These are a few of the insults that are thrown into Jasmine's face almost every day in our foster care group home, but that's not where it ends.

I've been in the same group homes with Jasmine for over a year and I've come to realize that everybody takes their anger out on her. One girl will get into an argument with Jasmine, then that girl's friends will make it into a bigger argument. Most of the time, she ends up getting jumped.

One time they trashed Jasmine's room after she got into a fight with them. They ripped down her posters and pulled the head off her stuffed animal. They threw her clothes into a pile and pissed on them, and then they peed on her bed.

From that time on, I felt pity for Jasmine.

I have to admit that I haven't always treated Jasmine much better. Many times I've taken my anger out on her.

I was quick to argue with Jasmine because I knew the rest of the girls would be on my side. It made me feel superior to her. Sometimes I was glad to see her get picked on, as long as it wasn't me who they were dissing.

I stopped teasing her after I realized why I was doing it. When I was living back home, I got verbally trashed by my father all the time. He would call me "trash" and "fat and lazy."

> ## MOST SCAPEGOATS HAVE BEEN ABUSED ALL THEIR LIVES AND DON'T KNOW HOW TO STOP IT.

I realized that many kids who've been verbally abused or neglected by family members will take out their anger on weaker kids. It's a vicious cycle that needs to be stopped.

But other girls in my group home don't seem to realize why they do it, or make up excuses. It's easy for them to pick on Jasmine because everyone is already against her.

Most of the girls say that Jasmine starts it off by getting an attitude with them. I always point out that her attitude is a result of all the abuse she takes.

"Why should she be nice all of a sudden?" I ask the girls. "She knows that in the next five minutes you'll be getting your attitude with her."

Jasmine was much weaker and quicker to have a breakdown in our previous group home. She's much stronger now because of all of the stuff she's been through. She's learned how to stick up for herself. But because she had a weak personality before, people are used to taking advantage of her. Even the new girls talk down to Jasmine.

Most scapegoats have been abused all their lives and don't know how to stop it. A lot of times I actually see Jasmine feeding into it. If people aren't dissing her or arguing with her, then they're not talking to her at all. So she'll do things to start arguments. Maybe scapegoats like the negative attention. Maybe the negative attention is better than no attention at all.

The abuse Jasmine takes won't end soon. Maybe she won't get into any more fights, but she'll still be the one excluded from conversations. Girls will still dis her and make her feel unwanted, but next time I plan to be on her side.

Angela Rutman *was 16 when she wrote this story. On leaving foster care, she attended college and majored in English.*

THiNk ABOUT iT

▶ Angela admits that she teased Jasmine in the past. She says it gave her a sense of superiority. Have you ever teased or bullied someone? Why did you do it?

▶ What is a scapegoat? Why do people make scapegoats of others? What kinds of people end up as scapegoats?

▶ Angela plans to defend Jasmine the next time someone teases her. Think of someone you know who gets teased or bullied. What could you say or do in the future to help that person and stop the bullying?

THere Are 20 SIDes TO every STORY

By Stephany Cover

Last year I was sitting in class beside my friend writing notes to her on my hand. One note said "I hate Michael" and, unluckily for me, a girl named Erica saw it. For some twisted and sick reason she went and told Meredith, the school bully, that I had a note on my hand that said "I hate Meredith." And it didn't stop there. Erica told her friends that I said Meredith was fat and ugly. I had never even met the girl!

The next day, friends of Erica and Meredith kept coming up to me and asking me if I really did say those things about Meredith. Someone told me that Meredith wanted to fight me! I couldn't believe it. Why was Erica doing this to me?

Then it came to me. Erica and I hadn't been getting along ever since I started going out with this guy she liked. "How stupid can you get?" I thought. "She's doing this because of a guy!"

I realized that this "I said, she said" thing was making life difficult. There were too many people involved. I had to talk to Meredith. This was going to be tough. It was like facing Goliath himself! But if I didn't face her now and try to explain everything then there was sure to be a fight. I was scared. You would be too.

I asked one of my friends who did know her to introduce me to Meredith. She was confused and upset and didn't know who to believe, me or Erica. Meredith and I talked about it for a while. I told her my side of the story. Then she told me she didn't want to fight me because she was already in a lot of trouble in school. But there were so many people besides Erica involved in this. We had to find a way to stop the rumors.

WE HAD TO FIND A WAY TO STOP THE rumors.

The next day Meredith and I decided to go to the dean's office. We tried to explain everything to the dean in the order that it happened. He thought it was complicated because of all the people involved. We had to find a way to break it down so that everybody could see how it all started. Not only were Meredith's friends pressuring her to fight me, but my friends were pressuring me into fighting Meredith. They all said that if Meredith came up to me and started accusing me of things, that I should just pop her! Meredith and I had to make our friends see that all of that talk was ridiculous because Erica started the whole thing.

The dean, Meredith, and I came up with an idea: a conflict-resolution group. The next day Meredith and I went around to all the people whom Erica had involved in her little gossip triangle of lies. We told them that the dean would like to talk to everyone involved. The dean said that everyone had to be in the room at the same time. We all sat around this huge round table. Each person then had her chance to tell her piece of the story. I thought that no one should be able to change her story and the dean agreed. This was to make sure that nothing became more complicated than it already was.

When we finally started, everyone had a different story. Some said that the message on my hand was totally different than what Erica had originally told them. There were even stories about other people that they knew, besides Meredith. Each person in the room was given time to question the person who was talking about her part of the story. There were questions like, "Who told you this, Erica or Stephany?"

It became quite clear during all these stories that Erica had made the whole thing up. When my friend told everyone what the note on my hand really said, it was even more obvious. But Erica kept denying the whole thing. She kept saying that the only reason they were doing this was because they wanted to see her get jumped. But Erica must have been lying. These were her friends taking my side. Erica still insisted that I said those things. I thought to myself, "She must really hate me."

Everyone finally learned the truth about it, and *oh, my, gawd* was Erica in trouble: two weeks of detention from the dean. Meredith and I became friends and to me she was no longer a threat. The conflict-resolution group did help a lot because we ended up not fighting over a situation that now seems immature to me.

This process can work for nearly anyone. Get everyone's cooperation and find a teacher, counselor, or someone else you can talk to. Sometimes it is better to talk things out rather than to just fight. It brings us one step closer to being mature adults.

I feel this is a successful way to solve problems of any kind, but you have to make the decision to do it on your own. People have to realize that not wanting to fight doesn't make you weak. I guess the only person who really should be mad at me is Michael, because he was the one the note was really about.

Stephany Cover *was 15 when she wrote this story. She majored in business management at the University of California, Berkeley.*

THiNk ABOUT iT

▶ Do rumors or gossip get out of control at your school? Have you ever been affected by rumors or gossip? How do they lead to conflict?

▶ Stephany says, "People have to realize that not wanting to fight doesn't make you weak." Do you agree or disagree with her? Where does real strength come from?

WHO'S THE REAL "PROBLEM CHILD"?

By Marcus J. Howell

"Problem children," "hoodlums," "people who end up in jails or mental homes"—these are some of the labels that are tagged on foster youth from the day we enter care.

I am not a label. I am a person who has been labeled all my life and I've always fought it. I've grown to hate hearing, "Oh, he's just a foster kid, he doesn't know what he's doing" or "Those two are mine, and, oh him? He's just a foster kid."

When people say these things, they have no idea how much it hurts the person they're speaking about. The term "foster child" itself, if said in a certain way, becomes a put-down.

Walking around the halls of my school, I hear the jokes of my classmates. Things like: "Group home kid" (in reference to someone who acts up in class) and "You delinquent" (in reference to someone in foster care). Phrases used when speaking (most of the time) behind our backs.

One memory that stands out the most is when I overheard a girl talking about her foster sister in the school lunchroom.

"Yeah, and that little punk dared to talk to my mother that way. Is it my mother's fault that her father molested her? Was it my mother's fault he beat her too? Why should that little delinquent get the same as the rest of us? We are my mother's real children, not her. She probably liked her father molesting her, that little group home slut."

My friends who knew I was in foster care looked at the girl, then looked at me, and waited to see what I was going to say. They were as shocked as I was.

I looked across at her and anger swelled in me. How could she say such a thing? How could she speak that way about someone else's personal life? I could see that she hated her foster sister bitterly. I wondered what kind of family could allow such hate toward a family member. And I knew that I had never, in all my years in foster care, met a person so bent on cruelty toward another.

I could nearly taste the acid in my stomach. Harsh words filled my head as I looked at the girl, but I didn't say them. Instead, without so much as a word or a second look, I stood up and left the table.

Before that moment, I used to envy the "normal" people who were given the chance to live with their own blood. But after that day, when I saw the hate that came from a "normal" family's life, I looked at my own world and was content.

Marcus J. Howell, *17 when he wrote this story, lived in foster care for most of his childhood before returning to live with his father.*

THiNk ABOUT iT

- Do you belong to a group of people who have been labeled by others? How has that affected you?

- Have you overheard people making hateful remarks about others? How did you react?

A DIFFERENT KIND OF FRIEND

By LaToya Souvenir

It was my first day at a new high school. I walked into math class and took a seat in the back of the room. The teacher wore an immaculately ironed, light-blue dress shirt and dark brown dress pants, but instead of a nice pair of shoes to complement the outfit, he was wearing a cheap pair of sneakers. Then I noticed the thick glasses and the pocket protector overflowing with pens.

"Of all the math teachers in this school, why did I have to be assigned the *Nerd Man?*" I said to no one in particular. I couldn't help it—this guy was prime dissing material.

No sooner had I said it than I heard someone laugh. Sitting next to me was a Puerto Rican girl with curly, dark brown hair and braces laughing her head off.

What was her problem? I hadn't said anything that hilarious. "Either she had a little too much to drink this morning or she's just ditsy," I thought. I definitely didn't like her. She had just a little too much sense of humor for me.

"Is this your first year in this school?" she asked when she finally stopped laughing.

"Yes," I said as rudely as I could. I had already made up my mind she and I were never going to become friends.

"Are you a freshman?"

"No." I thought that if I gave her only one-word answers she would leave me alone.

"What school did you transfer from?"

"Maxwell."

"Where's that?"

"Brownsville, that's my zoned school," I said, rolling my eyes.

"Brownsville, that's where I live," she said. "I thought Thomas Jefferson was the zoned school for Brownsville."

"Maxwell is too," I told her as the teacher asked us to be quiet. Then it hit me: "Wait a minute, where did you say you lived?"

"Brownsville."

Except for this one girl who used to live on my block, I had never seen Puerto Rican people around my way before.

Knowing that she lived in my neighborhood gave me a feeling of security in this strange, new school. Her name was Lisa, which surprised me. It was so un-Spanish. Didn't they all have names like Maria, Rosa, or Blanca?

After that, Lisa and I would say hi when we saw each other in the hallway. We would talk in class. She was easy to talk to and we always made each other laugh. But I saw no reason for us to become more than school friends.

Her being Puerto Rican was still in the back of my mind. Other than a girl named Rosa in junior high school, I had never even met a Puerto Rican person before. My elementary school, junior high, zoned high school, my neighborhood—even my church—were all predominantly black. I rarely had the chance to interact with people of other races. I was used to being around my own people and I wasn't about to change.

Since Rosa from junior high was the only Puerto Rican person I had ever known, I assumed that all Puerto Rican girls were like her: rice-and-beans-eating, *"mira, mira"*—("look, look")—yelling girls who went around cleaning up after their men all day.

I started to ask myself if Lisa was going to be like that. What if she wanted to hug and kiss each time we saw each other? I was not down with that. What if Lisa spoke Spanglish and I couldn't understand her? What was I supposed to call her—Hispanic? Latino? Latina? Puerto Rican? Would she be insulted if I picked the wrong one? I imagined that because she was of a different race, I would have to speak to her differently.

For all of sophomore year, Lisa and I remained casual acquaintances. I knew that she lived in Brownsville, but I didn't know where. Because I had never seen her before, I assumed that she didn't live anywhere near me.

In junior year our schedules changed and we no longer had the same math class. We hardly ever saw each other. Then one day, on my way home from school, I saw Lisa.

It turned out that we only lived a few blocks apart and had never once stumbled across each other. After that discovery, we began to travel to and from school together.

Besides going to the same school and living in the same neighborhood, it turned out that the two of us had a lot in common. We are both the oldest in our families, both have brothers, both live in houses (not apartments) with both our parents. Recently, we discovered that both our mothers have a ridiculous rule about not allowing us to have a guy in our bedroom.

Lisa and I started hanging out together in and out of school. We would often walk to class together or meet up afterwards. I introduced her to my friends and family, and she introduced me to hers. We even made new friends together.

But it wasn't always easy. When I told my mom about my new friend she just said, "Oh." She never said anything more, but she didn't have any Puerto Rican friends and I don't think she was particularly thrilled that I did.

One time Lisa and I were walking in my neighborhood when my friend Mel called me over. After a couple minutes, he looked at Lisa and asked, "What's she doing over here? You just wanna show her what a ghetto looks like?"

"No," I said, looking at him like he was stupid. "She lives over here." This wasn't the first time people had made ignorant comments about Lisa.

> I WAS USED TO BEING AROUND MY OWN PEOPLE AND I WASN'T ABOUT TO CHANGE.

"Well, how come I never seen her before?"

"Maybe you just wasn't looking."

At first I was shocked at how prejudiced so many of my friends were, but by this point I was just tired. I was tired of them acting like she was some sort of specimen on display. She was a person just like the rest of us.

I understood where it came from, because I had a little bit of that garbage in my head also. But luckily I had started to overcome it.

Over time, Lisa and I became inseparable. During senior year, I actually started hanging out at her house.

I really like her family (not that I don't like my own). Lisa's father spends time with his children, he jokes around and plays with them, and they talk to each other. With her mother, she can talk about anything.

SHE WAS A PERSON JUST LIKE THE REST OF US.

The entire family eats dinner together, which I think is wonderful. Every year for Christmas, they choose the house of an aunt, uncle, or grandparent, and everyone spends the day there, opening presents and singing carols. Someone even dresses up as Santa Claus and passes out the gifts. I wish my family did those things.

At first I would go over there maybe once every two weeks. Now I'm over there almost every day. I often go shopping with her mother, and sometimes we go visit her mother's friends. Her father has even begun to call me his "adopted daughter." Everyone on her block knows me. It's like I live there.

Lisa and her family have destroyed my stereotypes about Puerto Rican people. She doesn't want a kiss every time we see each other. In fact, she never wants a kiss. She speaks as much English as I do, and like me, she speaks differently when she's at home.

It's been years since that day in math class and Lisa still listens to my problems no matter how silly they may seem, and no matter how late I may call. When I need someone to pour my heart out to, to help solve my problems, or to tell me how rude I'm acting, Lisa is always there.

Although it took me some time to realize it, Lisa is my true friend.

LaToya Souvenir *was 17 when she wrote this story. She majored in public administration in college.*

THiNk ABOUT iT

- LaToya says she was prejudiced against Lisa at first. Some of her prejudiced feelings came from her family. Does your family influence the way you view other races, cultures, or groups of people? What other things have influenced your views toward others?

- We all have prejudices or the potential to believe in stereotypes. How can people overcome their prejudices or learn to see beyond their stereotypes?

SHE'S COOL, SHE'S FUNNY, SHE'S GAY

By Sandra Leon

When I was younger, I never really cared about what other people had to say about homosexuals. But ever since my sister Sonia came out of the closet, I've been outspoken on the topic. Now I can't let the dumb remarks I hear about gay people go by without commenting on them.

I always knew my sister Sonia was gay and it never bothered me. But when she finally told my mother, we thought mom was going to scream at the top of her lungs. My mother raised us to think homosexuality was wrong and strange. She totally hated it. I thought mom would disown Sonia or at least try to force her to be straight.

She did neither. What she did do was withdraw from my sister's life. For a couple of weeks my mother totally ignored Sonia. It felt like there was always tension in the air—my mom and Sonia were like the same sides of a magnet because they repelled each other. Say my mom was going to the kitchen and Sonia was leaving at the same time. They would meet and then do a 180 to avoid each other. My mom would not step into the kitchen unless Sonia wasn't there and Sonia wouldn't leave the kitchen unless she was 100 percent sure Mom wasn't outside in the hallway.

Then one day my sisters and I were discussing a problem Sonia was having with her first lesbian relationship. My mother overheard and asked us what we were talking about. My little sister said bluntly, "Oh nothing, just that Sonia's got woman troubles." My mother's mouth opened wide but she didn't say a word. She just gave Sonia a how-could-you-talk-to-your-sisters-about-that look.

That night, my sisters and I told mom how we felt about Sonia's sexuality. It took a long time but we finally got through to her. At the end of the discussion, Mom told Sonia that even if she didn't agree with what Sonia "chose" to be, she would always love her.

My mom also told Sonia that whenever she had a problem she could always come to her and talk about it. Sonia can openly talk to my mother when she's hurting, no matter what she's hurting about.

I think it's great the way my mother has come to accept Sonia for who she is. Now I'm trying to get my friends to do that too. They're always asking me, "Why is she gay?" and "How does it feel to have a gay sister?" Then, they want to tell me how they feel about gay people.

So, every time I bring friends to my house now, Sonia is the first person I introduce them to. When we leave, I tell them, "That's my sister who is gay." Some of my friends just say, "Oh, she's the one? Well, she's nice." But others do a double take. "That's her? No way, get out of here, really?!"

The people who are surprised tell me that Sonia doesn't look gay or that she doesn't act like a gay person. I reply, "What does a gay person look like? How are they supposed to act?" After that, all they have left to say is, "Well, you know." I tell them, "No, I don't know," and ask them to explain themselves.

As a result, I've gotten into some heavy conversations about gay stereotypes with my friends. I couldn't believe some of the ideas they had about gay people. They told me that gay women dress and look masculine. That they act like men because that's what they want to be. Since my sister isn't like that, she couldn't be gay as far as they were concerned.

I tell them that their stereotypes just aren't true. As far as I know, my sister loves being a woman. She enjoys her femininity. Her being gay does not have anything to do with a secret desire to be a man—far from it. Sonia is gay because she enjoys the company of other women, physically as well as mentally. She's told me that, for her, a relationship between two women is deeper than that of a woman and a man.

Another thing that a lot of my friends believe is that gay people try to get straight people to become gay. Once a friend asked if she could stay at my house for a couple of days. I told her she could stay as long as she wanted, but she must be comfortable with my sister. She said, "Okay, as long as Sonia doesn't fall in love with me." I thought that was a very stupid thing for her to say. My sister doesn't chase after straight women. So I replied with sarcasm, "You're not her type, so please darling, don't flatter yourself."

HOW CAN YOU BE OPEN-MINDED ABOUT ONE ASPECT OF A PERSON AND CLOSE-MINDED ABOUT ANOTHER?

Some of my friends also feel that gay people have a negative view of the opposite sex. Not true. My sister has always had men for best friends. Just because she's not attracted to them sexually does not mean that she hates men.

I've found out that a lot of people who condemn discrimination based on race or religion or nationality act like discrimination against gay people is acceptable. Why is that? How can you be open-minded about one aspect of a person and close-minded about another? Even people who have been victims of discrimination themselves can be totally insensitive when it comes to gay people.

I don't understand people like that, but I can give them a piece of advice: open your eyes and ears, your minds and your hearts. My mother has and so have a lot of my friends. Knowing Sonia has taught them that you can't believe stereotypes.

Sandra Leon *was 17 when she wrote this story. She majored in English and American literature at New York University.*

THiNk ABOUT iT

- Sandra never really cared what people said about gay people until she found out her sister was gay. Then she started speaking up to defend gay people. Have you ever defended a group of people because you knew someone who was a part of that group?

- Sandra's friends have a lot of stereotypes about gay people. Where do stereotypes come from? What can be done to change them? What can you do?

- Sandra says that "a lot of people who condemn discrimination based on race or religion or nationality act like discrimination against gay people is acceptable." Do you know people who condemn certain kinds of discrimination but accept other kinds? Why do you think they do that?

BACK OFF: Peer Mediation Can Help

By Zainab Muhammad

"Where are you going?" I asked Shawn. We were in shop class and it was getting boring.

"I'm going to peer mediation," Shawn answered. "Since I am a peer mediator, I get to mediate whenever there is a fight."

I watched the teacher give him a pass and Shawn did not return for another two periods.

That's when I got the idea to join peer mediation. I figured it would be an easy way to get out of class. When I found out that you get some extra points on your transcript, I went to sign up that same day.

But after I joined, I stopped thinking about peer mediation as just a good way to cut class. I realized that it is also a very effective way to decrease violence—one that should be used in all schools.

I know some of you are saying to yourselves, "She is being unrealistic. Who's going to want to talk to some random students when they're about to get in a fight?" I understand where you're coming from.

In fact, in the past, if I was about to get into a fight, the last thing I would be thinking about is going to peer mediation.

But peer mediation can work. I know, from personal experience.

A while back, I got into a pretty serious argument with another girl in my class (I'll call her Vicki) and it was about to lead to a fight.

A boy in my class had called me some names, and I began insulting him back. Then Vicki butted in and said that I shouldn't have said anything to him. I told her to shut up.

I said some more words that I didn't want to say, and she did the same as well, and soon we were in a shouting match. I think I would have hit Vicki if she wasn't on the other side of the room.

I was too overcome with anger to stay in the room, so I left and went to the peer mediation office (not because of the fight but because I had to help with some paperwork).

Five minutes after I got there, Vicki came in saying the teacher had sent her down and that we had to get mediated.

Although we did not listen to some of the rules—like no shouting—we did make an agreement not to get in each other's way. That was three months ago and we haven't had any problems since.

Students can go to peer mediation on their own, but in most cases, they are sent there by the deans or teachers.

When students walk into the room, they sit face to face, but a big distance apart (about 8 feet). There are usually two student mediators who sit in between them so if anyone jumps up he or she can be restrained.

There is also a teacher present, but he or she usually doesn't do much. The student mediators explain the basic rules (no yelling, cursing, or rude behavior) and then one mediator asks who would like to go first.

When I got mediated, I was desperate to go first. I had a lot to say.

First I told Vicki that she was a terrible friend and that she should just stay away from me since she couldn't keep her mouth closed. I told her that although she had been a very nice person before, she had changed. I talked for like 10 minutes, while Vicki cried and banged on the desk like she wanted to do something bad.

Eventually, the teacher (who only mediated because the mediators were unable to calm us down) began to help us resolve the situation.

I was still quite mad at Vicki, but I had spent so much time yelling and whining that I had also begun to feel a little better.

Ordinarily, when I get into an argument, I leave saying, "I should have said this or that." But when I participated in mediation, I had more than enough time to say what I wanted to say and it made me feel better.

The teacher then told us we had to come up with an agreement—if we didn't, we would be suspended. So we agreed to respect and stay away from each other. Then we signed it and we haven't fought since.

That's when I decided that peer mediation might actually be a program that works.

I'm not saying peer mediation works all the time. There are still times when students make an agreement and don't stick to it. Other times two students will come to us with a problem and one of them will leave feeling hopeless because she didn't get the help she wanted, or because she's afraid she'll be called a snitch.

But peer mediation does give students a chance to talk to their peers about issues they're having in school—issues they may feel uncomfortable telling an administrator. I think all students know the frustration of trying and failing to get help from administrators and adult staff.

I think we need more programs where students can sit down and talk about problems, not only after a conflict, but whenever they feel a problem coming on and have no one to talk to about it.

If there were more creative programs like that, there'd be fewer fights in school.

Zainab Muhammad *was 16 when she wrote this story. She later attended community college.*

THiNk ABOUT iT

▶ Would peer mediation help with disputes you or other students have had in school? Why or why not?

▶ Zainab says that peer mediation allows students to tell other students their problems, because sometimes students don't want to tell adults. Why is talking to a student about a problem sometimes better than talking to an adult?

▶ The kids in mediation have to come up with an agreement or be suspended. But there's no punishment for breaking the agreement. Do you think most kids at your school would stick to an agreement like this? Why or why not?

MY SCHOOL IS LIKe A FAMILY

By T. Shawn Welcome

I used to go to a big high school and I hated it. It was cold and unfeeling—as close to being put in an institution as I ever want to get. The teachers only cared about the work. It seemed they could care less about any problems a student might be dealing with.

The students weren't much better. They were there to show off and try to be cool. I was dealing with a lot of personal problems at the time and going to a big, impersonal education facility with metal detectors, I.D. scanners, and hall passes wasn't helping me at all.

I started getting more and more depressed and began to cut classes. At one point, I stopped going to school altogether.

Meanwhile, my guidance counselor was trying to talk me into applying to a small alternative high school. She said it was a school that would allow me to work at my own pace and I wouldn't be as stressed as I was at the big school. She kept talking about how the teachers and students were on a first name basis, and that they had a class called Family Group, where people would talk to each other about their problems.

It all sounded good but I didn't feel like adjusting to a new school, new people, and a whole load of new work.

She tried to get me to apply there for about a year, but I wasn't budging. Then, in the 11th grade, I heard that my best friend, Eric, had applied and was accepted. He would tell me about how free the atmosphere was and how good some of the girls looked. I asked him to pick up an application for me, and, with my counselor's help, I filled it out.

It took a lot of hard work, but I was accepted.

It was a relief to know that I was finally going to get away from my old school and be able to start a new life. I wanted to leave all my personal and scholastic problems behind. Leaving my old school symbolized the beginning of a new era for me.

All the new students had to go to an orientation during the summer where we played a bunch of get-to-know-each-other games. So by the first day of school we already knew each other. My new school has fewer than 400 students (my old one has about 3,500), so everyone gets to know each other quickly anyway.

My first month wasn't what I'd expected. When I heard the word *alternative*, I thought that there would be a lot of people who were put there because they had a record of fighting or who had been expelled from other schools. It wasn't like that.

> I FELT AT HOME THERE ALMOST RIGHT AWAY.

I felt at home there almost right away. I was finally getting what I didn't have at my old school— a feeling that I belonged. There wasn't that much fronting going on. I found myself talking to other students about my personal life and taking their advice.

Once we were in class and I was talking about my problems with my father when I suddenly got very emotional. I got up and left the room so the others wouldn't see me cry. Qwana, another student who didn't even know me that well, came out into the hall after me and held me. I never experienced anything like that at my old school—I don't think anyone did. I didn't even know it was possible.

I didn't know there were other ways of teaching, either. For one thing, the classes are not overcrowded. And the teachers don't just write on the blackboard and have you copy the notes.

In Spanish class, for example, the learning is interactive. Frank, one of my Spanish teachers, would write the verbs that we were learning that week on the blackboard and then break the class up into groups of four or five. Each group would have to work together to make sentences with the verbs and the adjectives that we had studied the week before. Then we'd have a contest to see which group made the best sentences. It made you forget you were in class and helped you get to know your peers better.

The teachers are good people, too. They have the rare ability to care about their students' lives while still doing their job. Michelle teaches Family Group, which is kind of like homeroom. She understands that students sometimes have problems and she tries to help as much as she can, but she also knows how to get under your skin until you do things right.

My friend Sean, nicknamed Whitey, would miss some days of school and Michelle would nag him to make up his work. After he spoke to her and she understood that he had financial problems, she helped him get a job in the school. That way she was able to keep an eye on him and he could make some money. Sometimes she gets on our nerves with the nagging, but the people who love you will always annoy you once in a while.

Gus, who teaches gym, is another teacher who's really cool. When I was in his class, he always seemed like he was a friend more than a teacher. He would go out of his way to help me with my work and he used to lift weights and play basketball and volleyball with us. Every time I see him now, he's always calling me the future writer. He's always saying that he's going to see me on television reporting the news some day. Gus makes me feel good about who I am.

I always feel respected and cared for by my teachers. If I don't, I'll tell them and we'll resolve it. I remember when Marion, one of my teachers, interrupted me when I was talking one time in class. I didn't say anything to her but she could tell that I was upset. She approached me in the hallway and said that she didn't mean to cut me off, but time was running out. I accepted her apology. To tell you the truth, I was shocked that she took the time to apologize to a student.

Now that I'm about to graduate, I realize that many things about my school have helped to make me a better person. Number one is that I always feel like I'm important there. The teachers care about me and not just the work I do.

But it isn't just that we have a special bond with our teachers. We also have a special bond with each other.

In November, we had a Thanksgiving lunch where everyone brought food from their own ethnic backgrounds. I didn't think it was going to work, because if you had asked people at my old high school to bring food to a luncheon, people would've been starving. But to my surprise, the attendance was nearly 100 percent. There were about seven or eight tables decorated with tablecloths, eating utensils, and lots of food.

People were dishing out food for each other and asking them to taste what they brought. There was Italian food, Spanish food, American food, West Indian food—you name it.

"Who made that macaroni salad, because it tastes mad good?"

"Pass me the salad!"

"Try some of my *pasteles*." (A Spanish food.)

"Yo Rose, get me a piece of turkey, please?"

This is what you were hearing all day. I felt like we were a real family.

T. Shawn Welcome *was 19 when he wrote this story. He is now assistant principal of an alternative high school in New York City.*

THiNk ABOUT iT

▐▶ Would you like to go to a school like T. Shawn's? What could be done to bring students closer together in your school?

▐▶ Have you ever looked for a family outside of your biological family? Were you successful in finding it?

Glossary

AWOL: leaving without permission ("Absent Without Leave")

Bin Laden: Osama Bin Laden, the Islamic terrorist suspected of organizing the attacks against the United States on September 11, 2001.

blunt: marijuana rolled into a cigar

chill: to relax, calm down

crib: a house or apartment

dis, dissed: to disrespect someone

down: to be a part of something

foster care: a system of foster homes and group homes where young people live if their parents can't properly care for them

foster home: a private home where foster youth live with a family

front, fronting: to put up a front, to be fake

group home: a residence where groups of foster youth live, mainly older kids

herb: an unpopular kid, a nerd

homophobic: afraid of gay people

mad: a lot of, very

oreo: black on the outside, white on the inside; an insult to a black person

peoples: friends

rank on: to tease or make fun of someone

Spanglish: a blend of Spanish and English

squash: to stop something

sweat: to bother or annoy someone

transgendered: to strongly identify with the opposite sex, which can take the form of a boy dressing and acting like a girl, and vice versa

24/7: all the time

weed: marijuana

whack: silly, stupid

wild up, wild out: to act in a crazy, rowdy way

Looking for a Specific Topic?

About Educators for Social Responsibility (ESR)

ESR is a national, nonprofit organization that was founded in 1982. Its mission is to make teaching social responsibility a core practice in education so that young people develop the convictions and skills to shape a safe, sustainable, democratic, and just world.

ESR is a national leader in education reform. The organization's work spans the fields of social and emotional learning, character education, conflict resolution, diversity education, civic engagement, prevention programming, youth development, and secondary school improvement. ESR offers comprehensive programs, staff development, consultation, and resources for adults who teach children and young people in preschool through high school, in settings including K–12 schools, early childhood centers, and after-school programs.

ESR works in three broad areas:

- **Student skill development.** Works with teachers to help students develop social skills, emotional competencies, and qualities of character that increase interpersonal effectiveness and reduce intolerance and aggressive, anti-social behavior.

- **School and classroom climate.** Helps schools create safe, caring, respectful, and disciplined learning environments that promote healthy development and academic success for all students.

- **Response to social crises and world events.** Helps educators respond effectively to local, national, and international crises related to interpersonal and systemic violence, intolerance, and global conflicts and war.

Visit ESR's Web site (www.esrnational.org) for more information, to visit the Online Teacher Center, or to sign up for the free monthly e-newsletter.

You can contact ESR at:

Educators for Social Responsibility
23 Garden Street
Cambridge, MA 02138
Telephone: 617-492-1764 ext. 20
Fax: 617-864-5164
Email: educators@esrnational.org

About Youth Communication

Located in New York City, Youth Communication is a nonprofit youth development program whose mission is to teach writing, journalism, and leadership skills. The teenagers trained by Youth Communication, most of whom are New York City public high school students, become writers for two teen-written magazines, *YCteen* (formerly *New Youth Communications*), a general-interest youth magazine, and *Represent*, a magazine by and for young people in foster care. The stories in this anthology were originally published in these two magazines.

Youth Communication was created in 1980 in response to a nationwide study that found that the high school press was characterized by censorship, mediocrity, and racial exclusion. Keith Hefner cofounded the program and has directed it ever since.

Each year, more than 100 young people participate in Youth Communication's school-year and summer journalism workshops. They come from every corner of New York City, and the vast majority are African-American, Latino, or Asian teens. The teen staff members work under the direction of several full-time adult editors in Youth Communication's Manhattan newsroom.

Teachers, counselors, social workers, and other adults circulate the magazines to young people in their classes, after-school youth programs, and agencies. They distribute 70,000 copies of *YCteen* each month during the school year, and 10,000 bimonthly copies of *Represent*. Teachers frequently tell the Youth Communication staff that teens in their classes—including students who are ordinarily resistant to reading—clamor for these publications. For the teen writers, the opportunity to reach their peers with important self-help information, and with accurate portrayals of their lives, motivates them to create powerful stories.

Running a strong youth-development program, while simultaneously producing quality teen magazines, requires a balance between a process that is sensitive to the complicated lives and emotions of the teen participants and one that is intellectually rigorous. That balance is sustained in the writing/teaching/editing relationship, which is the core of Youth Communication's program.

The teaching and editorial process begins with discussions between the adult editors and the teen staff, during which they seek to discover the stories that are both most important to each teen writer and potentially most appealing to the magazines' readers.

Once topics have been chosen, students begin the process of crafting their stories. For a personal story, that means revisiting events from the past to understand their significance for the future. For a commentary, it means developing a logical and persuasive argument. For a reported story, it means gathering information through research and interviews. Students look inward and outward as they try to make sense of their experiences and the world around them, and to find the points of intersection between personal and social concerns. That process can take a few weeks or a few months. Stories frequently go through four, five, or more drafts as students work on them under the guidance of editors in the same way that any professional writer does.

Many of the students who walk through Youth Communication's doors have uneven skills as a result of poor education, living under extremely stressful conditions, or coming from homes where English is a second language. Yet, to complete their stories, students must successfully perform a wide range of activities, including writing and rewriting, reading, discussion, reflection, research, interviewing, and typing. They must work as members of a team, and they must accept a great deal of individual responsibility. They learn to read subway maps, verify facts, and cope with rejection. They engage in explorations of truthfulness and fairness. They meet deadlines. They must develop the boldness to believe that they have something important to say, and the humility to recognize that saying it well is not a process of instant gratification, but usually requires a long, hard struggle through many discussions and much rewriting.

It would be impossible to teach these skills and dispositions as separate, disconnected topics such as grammar, ethics, or assertiveness training. However, the staff has found that students make rapid progress when they are learning skills in the context of an inquiry that is personally significant to them, and that they think will benefit their peers.

Writers usually participate in the program for one semester, though some stay much longer. Years later, many of them report that working at Youth Communication was a turning point in their lives—that it helped them acquire the confidence and skills they needed for success in their subsequent education and careers. Scores of Youth Communication's graduates have overcome tremendous obstacles to become journalists, writers, and novelists. Hundreds more are working in law, education, business, and other careers.

You can contact Youth Communication at:

Youth Communication
224 West 29th Street
New York, NY 10001
Telephone: 212-279-0708
Fax: 212-279-8856
Email: info@youthcomm.org

Further Reading and Resources

Big City Cool: Short Stories About Urban Youth, edited by M. Jerry Weiss and Helen S. Weiss (New York: Persea Books, 2002). What is it like to grow up in the big city, surrounded by nonstop sizzle and endless opportunity? In these 14 compelling stories, young people of all backgrounds—from immigrant to native born, from privileged to poor—make their way in this glamorous yet risky world.

Breathing Underwater, by Alex Flinn (New York: HarperCollins Children's Books, 2002). In this novel, 16-year-old Nick hits his girlfriend and is sentenced by a judge to attend a weekly family violence class. He also has to keep a journal in which he writes about his anger and his abusive father.

Friends, Cliques, and Peer Pressure: Be True to Yourself, by Christine Wickert Koubek (Berkeley Heights, NJ: Enslow Publishers, 2002). This book explores teen friendship and popularity, and how to choose friends based on your own values.

Give a Boy a Gun, by Todd Strasser (New York: Simon & Schuster Books for Young Readers, 2002). This novel tells the story of two high school sophomores who have been harassed, beaten up, and cursed out by jocks at their high school. Finally, to get revenge, they steal guns from their neighbor and storm a school dance.

Mean Chicks, Cliques, and Dirty Tricks: A Real Girl's Guide to Getting Through the Day with Smarts and Style, edited by Erika V. Shearin Karres (Avon, MA: Adams Media Corporation, 2004). This is a girl's guide to coping with mean girls. It uses the words of real girls to explore how the meanness may get started, forms it may take, and how to stop it.

Paint Me Like I Am: Teen Poems from WritersCorps, **edited by Bill Aguado (New York: HarperTempest, 2003).** This is a collection of poems on such topics as race, drugs, abuse, and self-image by teens who have taken part in writing programs run by a national nonprofit organization called WritersCorps.

Please Stop Laughing at Me, **by Jodee Blanco (Avon, MA: Adams Media Corporation, 2003).** This memoir describes how one child was excluded, and sometimes physically abused, by her classmates from elementary school through high school. It explores what it means to be an outcast.

Teen Angst? Naaah . . . : A Quasi-Autobiography, **by Ned Vizzini (New York: Laurel-Leaf, 2002).** This memoir recounts one teen's life in junior high and high school as he copes with issues that all teens (and ex-teens) can relate to: school, parents, cliques, friends, and more.

Teen Cyberbullying Investigated: Where Do Your Rights End and Consequences Begin? **by Thomas A. Jacobs, J.D. (Minneapolis, MN: Free Spirit Publishing, 2010).** This book presents a collection of landmark court cases involving teens and charges of cyberbullying, and helps young people understand what it is, recognize when they may be its victims or perpetrators, and learn tactics for successfully dealing with it.

Teen Violence, **edited by Scott Barbour (San Diego, CA: Greenhaven Press, 1998).** This book presents opposing viewpoints on the issue of teen violence, discussing how serious the problem may be, its causes, and ways to reduce it.

What Do You Stand For? For Teens, **by Barbara A. Lewis (Minneapolis, MN: Free Spirit Publishing, 2005).** This book invites teens to explore and practice honesty, kindness, empathy, integrity, tolerance, patience, respect, and more. Dilemmas challenge readers to think about, discuss, and debate positive traits. Activities invite them to explore what they stand for. True stories profile real kids who exemplify positive traits.

resources FROM YOUTH COMMUNICATION

Fighting the Monster: Teens Write About Confronting Emotional Challenges and Getting Help, **edited by Al Desetta (New York: Youth Communication, 2004).** This book contains 39 true stories by teens about getting help for depression, cutting, sexual abuse, domestic violence, substance abuse, eating disorders, bereavement, promiscuity, uncontrolled anger, and many other topics. Teens describe what worked for them, including self-help, therapy, and medication.

The Heart Knows Something Different: Teenage Voices from the Foster Care System, **edited by Al Desetta (New York: Persea Books, 1996).** Fifty-one powerful stories by foster youth which explore family, living in the system, personal reflection, and looking to the future.

Out With It: Gay and Straight Teens Write About Homosexuality, **edited by Philip Kay, Andrea Estepa, and Al Desetta (New York: Youth Communication, 1996).** Sensitive issues of teen sexuality, coming out, homophobia, and relationships with family and friends are explored in articles authored by teens. Includes a 25-page "Resources for Teachers" section.

Starting With I: Personal Essays by Teenagers, **edited by Andrea Estepa and Philip Kay (New York: Persea Books, 1997).** "Who am I and who do I want to become?" Thirty-five stories examine this question through the lenses of race, ethnicity, gender, sexuality, family, and more. Free Teacher's Guide is also available.

The Struggle to Be Strong: True Stories by Teens About Overcoming Tough Times, edited by Al Desetta and Sybil Wolin (Minneapolis, MN: Free Spirit Publishing, 2000). In 30 first-person stories, teens tell how they faced and overcame major life obstacles. Readers learn about seven resiliencies—insight, independence, relationships, initiative, creativity, humor, and morality—that everyone needs to triumph over adversity.

Things Get Hectic: Teens Write About the Violence That Surrounds Them, edited by Philip Kay, Andrea Estepa, and Al Desetta (New York: Touchstone, 1998). Violence is commonplace in many teens' lives, whether from bullying, gangs, dating, or family relationships. Hear the experiences of victims, perpetrators, and witnesses through more than 50 real-world stories.

YCteen, a general-interest teen magazine.

Represent: The Voice of Youth in Foster Care, a magazine written by and for young people in foster care.

In addition, Youth Communication publishes dozens of booklets on a wide range of youth issues. See www.youthcomm.org for more information.

For ordering information, contact Youth Communication (see page 135).

Index

About the Editor

Al Desetta, M.A., is the editor of numerous books for young adults, including *The Struggle to Be Strong: True Stories by Teens About Overcoming Tough Times* (Free Spirit Publishing, 2001) and *The Heart Knows Something Different: Teenage Voices from the Foster Care System* (Persea Books, 1996). He is an editor at Youth Communication, a youth development organization in New York that teaches writing, journalism, and leadership skills to teens. He has served as instructor in the program's juvenile prison writing project, as editor of the organization's general interest teen magazine, *New Youth Connections*, and as founding editor of *Represent*, a nationwide magazine written by young people in foster care. Under his leadership, *Represent* received journalism awards from the Child Welfare League of America and the Casey Journalism Center for Children and Families. During the 1990–91 academic year, Desetta was a Charles H. Revson Fellow at Columbia University.

Other Great Books from Free Spirit

Fighting Invisible Tigers
Stress Management for Teens (Revised & Updated Third Edition)
by Earl Hipp
This book offers proven techniques that teens can use to deal with stressful situations in school, at home, and among friends. They'll find current information on how stress affects health and decision making and learn stress-management skills to handle stress in positive ways—including assertiveness, positive self-talk, time management, relaxation exercises, and much more. Filled with interesting facts, student quotes, and fun activities, this book is a great resource for any teen who's said, "I'm stressed out!" For ages 11 & up.
144 pp.; softcover; 2-color; illust.; 6"x 9"

GLBTQ*
The Survival Guide for Gay, Lesbian, Bisexual, Transgender, and Questioning Teens
(Revised & Updated 2nd Edition)
by Kelly Huegel, foreword by Phoenix Schneider, program director for The Trevor Project
Issues-based information and advice on coming out, prejudice, getting support, making healthy choices, school safety, workplace equality, and transgender expression. Written for young people who are beginning to question their sexual or gender identity, those who are ready to work for GLBTQ rights, and those who may need guidance or reassurance. For ages 13 & up.
240 pp.; softcover; 6"x 9"

Respect
A Girl's Guide to Getting Respect & Dealing When Your Line Is Crossed
by Courtney Macavinta and Andrea Vander Pluym
This smart, savvy book helps teen girls get respect and hold on to it no matter what. It covers topics they deal with daily, like body image, family, friends, the media, school, relationships, and rumors. Girls learn that respect is always within reach because it starts on the inside. For ages 13 & up.
240 pp.; softcover; 2-color; illust.; 7"x 9"

When Nothing Matters Anymore
A Survival Guide for Depressed Teens (Revised & Updated Edition)
by Bev Cobain, R.N.,C.
This book defines depression, describes the symptoms, and explains that depression is treatable. Personal stories from teens speak to readers' own feelings, concerns, and experiences. Teens learn how to take care of themselves and how treatment can help. Includes the latest information on medication, nutrition, and health; current resources; and a Q&A with questions teens have asked the author. For ages 13 & up.
160 pp.; softcover; 2-color; illust.; 6"x 9"

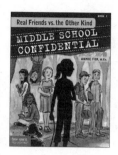

Real Friends vs. the Other Kind
(Middle School Confidential™ Series)
by Annie Fox, M.Ed.
The book offers insider information on making friends, resolving disputes, and dealing with other common middle school concerns—like gossip, exclusion, and cyberbullying. There's also expert advice on crushes, peer pressure, and being there for friends who need help. Filled with character narratives, quizzes, quotes from real kids, tips, tools, and resources, this book is a timely and engaging survival guide for the middle school years. For ages 11–14.
96 pp.; softcover; color illust.; 6"x 8"

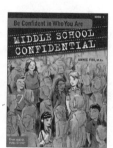

Be Confident in Who You Are
(Middle School Confidential™ Series)
by Annie Fox, M.Ed.
The book offers insider information on common middle school concerns and practical advice for being healthy, feeling good about who you are, and staying in control of your feelings and actions—even when the pressure is on. Filled with character narratives, quizzes, quotes from real kids, tips, tools, and resources, this book is a timely and engaging survival guide for the middle school years. For ages 11–14.
96 pp.; softcover; color illust.; 6"x 8"

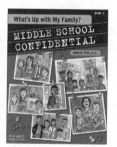

What's Up with My Family?
(Middle School Confidential™ Series)
by Annie Fox, M.Ed.
Six friends are trying to figure out how to negotiate family rules, routines, and responsibilities. Readers will find expert information for getting along with parents and handling common concerns that come up at home—including dealing with sibling conflicts, coping with divorce and life in a blended family, and being assertive when adults are genuinely unfair. For ages 11–14.
96 pp.; softcover; color illust.; 6"x 8"

Too Stressed to Think?
A Teen Guide to Staying Sane When Life Makes You Crazy
by Annie Fox, M.Ed., and Ruth Kirschner
When stress has the "survival brain" on overdrive, what happens to the "thinking brain"? How can teens learn to use the mind-body connection to stay cool and make smart choices when the pressure's on? Practical information, stress-lessening tools, quotes from real teens, and realistic scenarios help teens reduce or stop the stress and make decisions that won't leave them lamenting, "What was I thinking?" For ages 13 & up.
176 pp.; softcover; 6"x 9"

Kids with Courage
True Stories About Young People Making a Difference
by Barbara A. Lewis
Eighteen remarkable kids speak out, fight back, come to the rescue, and defend their beliefs. For ages 11 & up. *184 pp.; softcover; 6"x 9"*

Mad
How to Deal with Your Anger and Get Respect
by James J. Crist, Ph.D.
Teens with anger control problems will learn to manage their emotions so they stay out of trouble, improve relationships, and feel better about themselves. With dozens of practical anger-management tools and strategies, teens begin to understand their anger better and learn to avoid poor decisions and rash actions. For ages 13 & up. *160 pp.; softcover; 2-color; illust.; 6"x 9"*

What Do You Stand For? For Teens
A Guide to Building Character
by Barbara A. Lewis
This book invites teens to explore and practice honesty, kindness, empathy, integrity, tolerance, patience, respect, and more. Includes inspiring quotations, thought-provoking dilemmas, meaningful activities, and true stories about real kids who exemplify positive character traits. Updated resources point the way toward character-building books, organizations, programs, and Web sites. For ages 11 & up. *288 pp.; softcover; B&W photos and illust.; 8½"x 11"*

Life Lists for Teens
Tips, Steps, Hints, and How-Tos for Growing Up, Getting Along, Learning, and Having Fun
by Pamela Espeland
Lists organize your thinking, focus your energy, free up time in your day (and space in your brain), and give you confidence. No wonder everybody loves lists: making them, reading them, checking things off on them. In this book more than 200 powerful self-help lists cover topics ranging from health to cyberspace, school success to personal safety, friendship to fun. For ages 11 & up. *272 pp.; softcover; 6"x 9"*

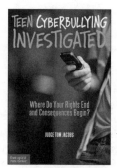

Teen Cyberbullying Investigated

Where Do Your Rights End and Consequences Begin?

by Thomas A. Jacobs, J.D.

This collection of landmark court cases involves teens and charges of cyberbullying and cyberharassment. Each chapter features a seminal cyberbullying case and resulting decision, asks readers whether they agree with the decision, and urges them to think about how the decision affects their lives. For ages 12 & up. *208 pp.; softcover; 6" x 9"*

They Broke the Law—You Be the Judge

True Cases of Teen Crime

by Thomas A. Jacobs, J.D.

This book invites teens to preside over a variety of real-life cases, to learn each teen's background, the relevant facts, and the sentencing options available. After deciding on a sentence, they find out what really happened—and where each offender is today. A thought-provoking introduction to the juvenile justice system. For ages 12 & up. *224 pp.; softcover; 6" x 9"*

What Are My Rights?

Q&A About Teens and the Law

(Revised & Updated 3rd Edition)

by Thomas A. Jacobs, J.D.

"Can I be prosecuted for comments I make online?" "When can I get a tattoo?" "Why can't I wear what I want to school?" Teens often have questions about the law, but they don't always know where to turn for the answers. This book gives them those answers, exploring more than 100 legal questions pertaining specifically to teens. The third edition includes fresh facts, updated statistics, and a new chapter addressing online issues from Facebook to file sharing. For ages 12 & up. *224 pp.; softcover; 6" x 9"*

Heart of a Warrior

7 Ancient Secrets to a Great Life

by Jim Langlas

The inspiration for this book comes from the ancient Korean history of the Hwarang—young student-warriors who worked to strengthen their spirits as well as their fighting skills. Author Jim Langlas, an educator and Taekwondo master, presents seven principles that are rooted in the long tradition of Taekwondo and are also tied to modern character education: courtesy, integrity, perseverance, self-control, indomitable spirit, community service, and love. For ages 12 & up. *160 pp.; softcover; 6" x 9"*

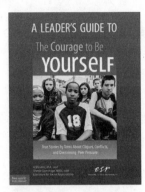

A Leader's Guide to
The Courage to Be Yourself
edited by Al Desetta, M.A. and Sherrie Gammage, M.Ed., with Educators for Social Responsibility
Twenty-six sessions based on the stories in *The Courage to Be Yourself* invite teens to go deeper into the stories and explore the themes of diversity, acceptance, and the roots and resolution of conflict. Includes activities, exercises, discussions, and reproducible handouts. For teachers, counselors, and other adults who work with youth in grades 7–12. *168 pp.; softcover; 8½"x 11"*

The Struggle to Be Strong
True Stories by Teens About Overcoming Tough Times
edited by Al Desetta, M.A., of Youth Communication, and Sybil Wolin, Ph.D., of Project Resilience
In 30 first-person accounts, teens tell how they overcame major life obstacles. Readers learn about seven resiliencies—insight, independence, relationships, initiative, creativity, humor, and morality—that everyone needs to overcome tough times. For ages 13 & up. *192 pp.; softcover; illust.; 6"x 9"*

Leader's Guide
by Sybil Wolin, Ph.D., and Al Desetta, M.A., and Keith Hefner of Youth Communication
For teachers, prevention specialists, and other adults who work with youth in grades 7–12. *176 pp.; softcover; 8½"x 11"*

Join the Free Spirit Teen Advisory Council

Do you like to read? Have you ever seen a book, a poster, a game, or an advertisement and thought, "I could make this better"? If so, apply for the Free Spirit Teen Advisory Council. Council members provide us with valuable feedback on things like the design, art, and content of our products. Apply today! For more information, go to www.freespirit.com/teens.

Interested in purchasing multiple quantities and receiving volume discounts?
Contact edsales@freespirit.com or call 1.800.735.7323 and ask for Education Sales.

Many Free Spirit authors are available for speaking engagements, workshops, and keynotes. Contact speakers@freespirit.com or call 1.800.735.7323.

For pricing information, to place an order, or to request a free catalog, contact:
Free Spirit Publishing Inc.
217 Fifth Avenue North • Suite 200 • Minneapolis, MN 55401-1299
toll-free 800.735.7323 • local 612.338.2068 • fax 612.337.5050
help4kids@freespirit.com • www.freespirit.com